Wild Orchids of South Carolina

Wild Orchids of South Carolina

A Popular Natural History

James Alexander Fowler

Introduction by Paul Martin Brown

University of South Carolina

Published in Columbia, South Carolina, by the
University of South Carolina Press

Manufactured in CHINA

09 08 07 06 05 5 4 3 2 1

Library of Congress Cataloging-in-Publication Data

Fowler, James Alexander, 1946–
Wild orchids of South Carolina : a popular natural history / James Alexander Fowler ; introduction by Paul Martin Brown.
p. cm.
Includes bibliographical references (p.).
ISBN 1-57003-566-0 (alk. paper)
1. Orchids—South Carolina—Identification. 2. Orchids—South Carolina—Pictorial works. I. Title.

QK495.O64F68 2005
584'.4'09757—dc22

2004054615

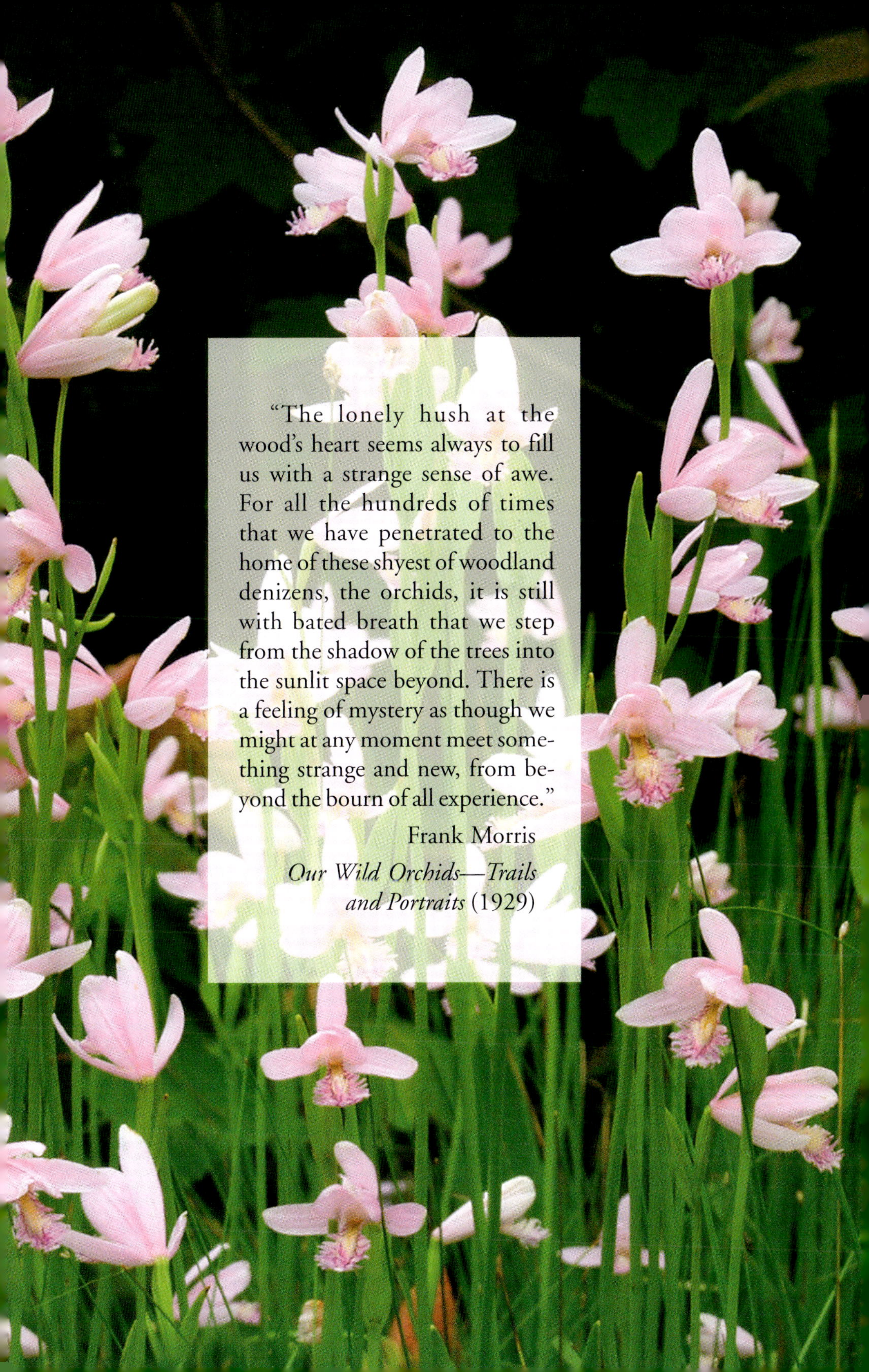

"The lonely hush at the wood's heart seems always to fill us with a strange sense of awe. For all the hundreds of times that we have penetrated to the home of these shyest of woodland denizens, the orchids, it is still with bated breath that we step from the shadow of the trees into the sunlit space beyond. There is a feeling of mystery as though we might at any moment meet something strange and new, from beyond the bourn of all experience."

Frank Morris

Our Wild Orchids—Trails and Portraits (1929)

Contents

By Common Name

Preface and Dedication

To this day, I don't know why I chose to write about wild orchids instead of other wild flowers—perhaps the orchids did the choosing.

For me, getting out into the field is more fun than any one person ought to be allowed. It's not without its more sobering moments, though—encountering terrible weather, snakes, irate swarms of hornets, biting flies, ticks, mosquitoes, and the ever present chigger. Not to mention the tens of thousands of miles I put on my vehicle chasing all over the state for this or that elusive bloom only to find that it had just finished blooming, or had not yet started to bloom, or no longer grew in the expected location.

My great-grandmother was the first person to encourage my interest in plants. She was a horticulturist with the U.S. Department of Agriculture in Florida back in the early 1900s and was responsible for introducing the honeydew melon and tung oil to the U.S. Every time I would see her, she would inquire about what I was growing or what I had seen growing in the woods. I seemed to have inherited from her a gift—the love of all living things, especially plants.

I remember, as a kid, bringing plants home from the woods and taking special care in digging the proper holes, spreading the roots, giving them water and the loving care I knew they needed to thrive. I must have been pretty good at it because my father once said that I could plant a baseball bat in the ground and it would sprout in a week.

Since it was they who inspired me, I dedicate this book to my father, John D. Fowler, Sr., and to my late great-grandmother Mattie MacLeod Matheson.

Acknowledgments

This book is a labor of love and is the result of input from many friends and acquaintances. My sincerest thanks go to people whom I now call my friends (in alphabetical order): Stan Bentley, John Brubaker, Mary Bunch, Sarah Davis, Frank Galloway, David McAdoo, Patrick McMillan, Virginia Meador, Bill Moye, John Nelson, Mark Pistrang, Richard Porcher, Annabelle Ritchey, Walter Shockley, Sandra Singer, John Snyder, April Stallings, Scott Stewart, Bill Stringer, Kelvin Taylor, and Ty Wilson.

Very special thanks must be given to my close friend and photographer buddy, Lucy Dueck, from whom I learned patience, humility, and a great deal about photographic composition and style.

I could not have persevered through the rigors of layout and review without the able help of Paul Martin Brown and Stan Folsom. Paul, a well-known author and orchid enthusiast, graciously volunteered to write the introduction and shared with me some of his favorite orchid habitats. Stan, a botanical artist and Paul's partner, reviewed the manuscript and offered many useful suggestions.

I am also grateful to the staff of the University of South Carolina Press. Alex Moore, Bill Adams, Linda Fogle, and Curtis Clark were instrumental in ensuring that the manuscript met the exacting requirements of the press by offering considerate and thoughtful guidance that made the task easy for this first-time author.

Finally, and definitely not least, I must thank my lifelong companion, Walter Ezell, for cheering me up when things seemed bleak, sharing with me the technical expertise that would get me through manuscript layout, and generally supporting my efforts when I had lingering doubts.

Without the generous help of the above named, this book would not have happened.

Introduction

South Carolina offers the orchid enthusiast a delightful potpourri of wild orchids distinctive to the southeastern United States. With fifty-five species currently found within the state, there is hardly a month in the year that does not have flowering plants of native orchids occurring somewhere in the forty-six counties. Because of South Carolina's varied habitats and topography, it is home to many of the more southerly species seen in Florida and the Gulf states, and within the mountains of the northern counties are the southern limits for several northern species. Such alluring species as *Arethusa bulbosa,* the dragon's-mouth, and *Platanthera psycodes,* the small purple fringed orchid, are among those northern species. Cautiously making its way up from the more southerly climes, *Habenaria quinqueseta,* Michaux's orchid, reaches the northern limit of its range in southeastern South Carolina.

The purpose of *Wild Orchids of South Carolina* is manyfold. Although this work is neither intended to be a comprehensive treatise nor a technical, scientifically oriented field guide, it is a popular account of one man's intoxicating obsession with wild orchids. As such, it becomes a valuable contribution to the knowledge of the orchids of South Carolina and an aesthetic presentation of the beauty and intricacies of these captivating flowers.

Nevertheless, in assembling a work such as this it becomes necessary to address certain taxonomic issues. The use of the genus *Gymnadeniopsis* for three species—*clavellata, integra,* and *nivea*—traditionally placed within the genera *Habenaria* and *Platanthera* is not novel. Rydberg created *Gymnadeniopsis* in 1901 to accommodate these three species because of their distinctive attributes. Unlike those of *Habenaria* and *Platanthera,* the columns of these species bear two pairs of appendages. In addition, several other characters, such as the formation of the roots, have been recognized, to some degree, by both Luer (1972, 1974,) and Sheviak (in *Flora of North America,* 2002). Brown (2003) revalidated the genus and has used it in *Wild Orchids of the Southeastern United States* (2004). Two recently described species new to science are included: *Spiranthes eatonii* and *Spiranthes sylvatica.* Both were originally found in Florida but range throughout the entire southeastern coastal plain from eastern Texas to southeastern Virginia.

Rarity is relative; what may be very common in one state or region may be exceedingly scarce elsewhere. Among the rarest orchids documented from within South Carolina would have to be counted *Platanthera integrilabia,* the monkey-face orchid, *P. peramoena,* the purple fringeless orchid, the aforementioned *Habenaria quinqueseta,* and *Arethusa bulbosa.* Unfortunately all of these species may not still be present in the state. From a global standpoint, the federally threatened *Isotria medeoloides,* the small whorled pogonia, is one of the rarest orchids to be found in North America. Extant populations of rare species in South Carolina certainly would include *Corallorhiza maculata,* the spotted coralroot, *Platanthera psycodes,* the small purple fringed orchid, and *Listera smallii,* Small's twayblade—all of which are found in greater abundance northward.

One of the joys, and to a few, the banes, of orchid taxonomy is the abundance of color, variation, and form within many of the species. Understanding variation within a species may make this less daunting and even add to the thrill of discovery. Apart from the genus *Spiranthes,* variation within many of the orchids of South Carolina is one of color and, upon rare occasions, growth forms. From the serious orchid enthusiasts' viewpoint, natural hybrids also fall into this category of aberrant individuals.

Many flowering plants, not just orchids, produce individuals with colors other than the normal range of the species. The color variation is generally the result of a genetic change, or mutation, within a single seed pod, or to a lesser extent, within individual ovules. Because so few seeds actually make it to mature, flowering plants, very few plants of the forms are usually noted. While some species, such as the pink lady's-slipper, *Cypripedium acaule,* have a natural range from palest blush pink to deep raspberry, it does produce a pure white form, forma *albiflorum,* which is lacking in all pink pigment. One clue is to carefully examine the sepals and petals as well as the prominent lip for lack of typical color. In this case they are green while the lip is purest white. As a rule, white-flowered forms, often incorrectly called albinos—those lacking in all color throughout the entire plant—will have paler leaves and stems. Purple-flowered species may produce clear pinks, oranges clear yellows, and so forth. Not all of these have been formally recognized with named forms, but most have. The other rarer variation would be that of growth forms—the production of an additional leaf, bracts replaced by full leaves, flowers simply reduced to colorful bracts, or multiple flowers. Some of the named forms that might be encountered while searching for orchids in South Carolina include:

Aplectrum hyemale, puttyroot orchid
forma *pallidum*—yellow-flowered form

Calopogon barbatus, bearded grass-pink
forma *albiflorus*—white-flowered form
forma *lilacinus*—lilac-flowered form, p. 15
Calopogon pallidus, pale grass-pink
forma *albiflorus*—white-flowered form, p. 23
Calopogon tuberosus, common grass-pink
forma *albiflorus*—white-flowered form, pp. 24, 26
Cleistes divaricata, rosebud orchid
forma *leucantha*—white-flowered form
Corallorhiza maculata, spotted coralroot orchid
forma *flavida*—yellow-stemmed form
forma *rubra*—red-stemmed form
Corallorhiza odontorhiza, autumn coralroot orchid
forma *flavida*—yellow-stemmed form
Corallorhiza wisteriana, Wister's coralroot orchid
forma *albolabia*—white-flowered form
forma *rubra*—red-stemmed form
Cypripedium acaule, pink lady's-slipper
forma *albiflorum*—white-flowered form, p. 48
forma *biflorum*—two-flowered form
Galearis spectabilis, showy orchis
forma *gordinierii*—white-flowered form
forma *willeyi*—pink-flowered form
Gymnadeniopsis clavellata, club-spur orchid
forma *slaughteri*—white-flowered form, p. 71
Hexalectris spicata, crested coralroot orchid
forma *albolabia*—white-flowered form
Liparis liliifolia, lily-leaved twayblade
forma *viridiflora*—green-flowered form
Listera australis, southern twayblade
forma *scottii*—many-leaved form
forma *trifolia*—3-leaved form
forma *viridis*—green-flowered form
Listera smallii, Small's twayblade
forma *variegata*—variegated-leaved form
Malaxis unifolia, green adder's-mouth orchid
forma *bifolia*—2-leaved form
forma *variegata*—variegated-leaf form

Platanthera blephariglottis, white fringed orchid
forma *holopetala*—entire-lip form
Platanthera cristata, crested fringed orchid
forma *straminea*—pale yellow-flowered form
Platanthera peramoena, purple fringeless orchid
forma *doddiae*—white-flowered form
Platanthera psycodes, small purple fringed orchid
forma *albiflora*—white-flowered form
forma *ecalcarata*—spurless form
forma *rosea*—pink-flowered form
forma *varians*—entire-lip form
Pogonia ophioglossoides, rose pogonia
forma *albiflora*—white-flowered form, pp. 154, 157
forma *brachypogon*—short-bearded form
Pteroglossaspis ecristata, crestless plume orchid
forma *flava*—yellow-flowered form
forma *purpurea*—dusky purple flowered form, pp. 162, 163
Spiranthes praecox, grass-leaved ladies'-tresses
forma *albolabia*—white-lipped form, p. 206
Tipularia discolor, crane-fly orchid
forma *viridifolia*—green-leaved form
Triphora trianthophora, three birds orchid
forma *albidoflava*—white-flowered form
forma *caerulea*—blue-flowered form

Natural hybrids present a different set of problems in field identification. It would be ideal if all natural hybrids occurred with both putative parents and presented a neat trio of plants. This is not always the case. More often than not, one of the suspected parents may either be a distance away, as the pollinator flies, or no longer be present at that specific site. Given the number of years it may take an individual orchid plant to flower from seed, the parent(s) may be missing through natural attrition. The good news is that there are very few potential hybrid combinations in the orchid flora of South Carolina. The bad news is those potential hybrids are within two complex groups. The orange/yellow/white fringed orchids, *Platanthera* spp., and the ladies'-tresses, *Spiranthes.* Four taxa occur in South Carolina in the former complex, and it is not at all unusual to find two or more growing sympatrically. This allows for several hybrid combinations. The best clue for determining the possibility of hybrids is if a nonconforming plant is found, look carefully about for potential parents and carefully compare such diagnostic characters as color, lip shape and position, sepal and petal shape and position, and, especially in *Platanthera,* spur length and shape of the nectary opening. Some of the possible hybrid combinations that may be found in South Carolina include:

Platanthera ×*beckneri,* Beckner's hybrid fringed orchis
(*P.* (*blephariglottis* var.) *conspicua* × *P. cristata*)
Platanthera ×*channellii,* Channell's hybrid fringed orchid
(*P. ciliaris* × *P. cristata*)
Platanthera ×*lueri,* Luer's hybrid fringed orchid
(*P.* (*blephariglottis* var.) *conspicua*) × *P. ciliaris*

Spiranthes ×*folsomii,* Folsom's hybrid ladies'-tresses
(*S. longilabris* × *S. odorata*)
Spiranthes ×*meridionalis,* southern hybrid ladies'-tresses
(*S. praecox* × *S. vernalis*)

In any geographic region there will be both cryptic species and unvouchered reports. South Carolina is not exempt from this, and four taxa have not been treated within the body of this work. Recent taxonomic and distributional work, in preparation for the treatment of the Orchidaceae in *Flora of North America* (2002), uncovered historical records for *Calopogon oklahomensis,* the Oklahoma grass-pink, and *Malaxis bayardii,* Bayard's adder's-mouth orchid—both additions to the flora of South Carolina. There are apparently no currently known sites for either of these two species, and the precise historical location of the *Calopogon* is unknown. However, herbarium specimens of Bayard's adder's-mouth have been annotated from several coastal plain counties. A recent report of *Platanthera flava* var. *herbiola,* the northern tubercled orchis, from north of Greenville remains to be substantiated, and the published record of *Zeuxine strateumatica,* the lawn orchid, is most likely the result of ephemeral plants growing within nursery stock. *Zeuxine,* a native of Asia, is widespread in Florida and is slowly insinuating itself within the flora of the southeastern coastal plain.

Species pairs offer an interesting look into possibilities of adaptation and evolution. These usually comprise two species that at one time were considered the same species or, in a few cases, comprise two superficially similar species. Adaptation is often necessary to take advantage of a specific pollinator or change in habitat. Five species pairs occur in South Carolina:

Calopogon barbatus, bearded grass-pink

Wide-spread along the Atlantic and eastern Gulf coastal plain

Small, early flowered; flowering sequentially

Calopogon oklahomensis, Oklahoma grass-pink

Recently described species primarily from the Midwest with historical records from the sandhills (presumed) of South Carolina and southwestern Georgia

Small, early flowered; flowering simultaneously

Cleistes bifaria, smaller rosebud orchid

Smaller in all proportions and range extends to the westward to the mountains and southwestward to the upper coastal plain

Cleistes divaricata, rosebud orchid

Larger in all proportions and confined to the immediate Atlantic coastal plain

Malaxis unifolia, green adder's-mouth orchid

Flower pedicels elongating forming a flat-topped raceme, lower flowers withering after anthesis; plants of both dry and damp locales; widespread in eastern North America

Malaxis bayardii, Bayard's adder's-mouth orchid

Flower pedicels uniform in length, lower flowers withering, but remaining after anthesis; plants of dry pine and granite barrens and sandy roadsides; rare and local; often misunderstood as critical identification criteria is the presence of auricles on the minute lip. Known in South Carolina from several herbarium records.

Platanthera blephariglottis var. *blephariglottis,* northern white fringed orchid

Widespread from Newfoundland to Georgia; spur moderate in length and lip lacking a distinct isthmus at the base

Platanthera blephariglottis var. *conspicua* (synonym: *Platanthera conspicua*), southern white fringed orchid

Restricted distribution from coastal North Carolina to eastern Texas (formerly); spur greatly exceeding lip length and with a distinct isthmus at the base of the lip; inland from the outer coastal plain

Platanthera ciliaris, yellow fringed orchid

Both species have a similar distribution, with *P. ciliaris* extending more inland to the foothills of the mountains. In photographs and drawings, the plants look strikingly the same, but in reality they are dramatically different in overall size. The spur on *P. ciliaris* exceeds the length of the lip and in *P. cristata* is less than the length of the lip. Differences also occur in the shape of the petals and opening of the nectary.

Platanthera cristata, crested fringed orchid

Of the five species pairs in South Carolina, this is the only pair that could regularly produce hybrids, *P.* ×*channellii.*

With the exception of a few species of *Spiranthes,* the remaining orchids found within South Carolina rarely present identification problems. The numerous forms and hybrids listed above are all fully described and most are illustrated in *Wild Orchids of the Southeastern United States.* Although range, habitat, and season are all helpful criteria, remember that the orchids rarely read books and therefore may just show up unannounced in new areas. Keep an open mind when searching for these sparkling gems in the wild, carefully digesting all of the available information, and you should be able to identify the wild orchids of South Carolina.

Paul Martin Brown

County Map of South Carolina

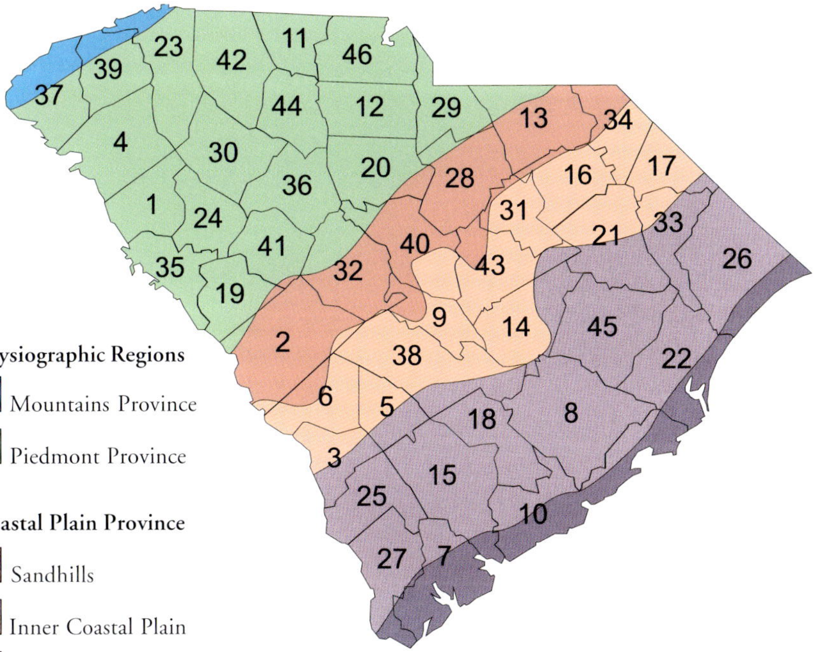

Physiographic Regions

- Mountains Province
- Piedmont Province

Coastal Plain Province

- Sandhills
- Inner Coastal Plain
- Outer Coastal Plain
- Maritime Strand

Based on Porcher and Rayner, *A Guide to the Wild-flowers of South Carolina*, 2001.

County Names

1 Abbeville *(4)
2 Aiken *(13)*
3 Allendale *(6)*
4 Anderson *(7)*
5 Bamberg *(6)*
6 Barnwell *(17)*
7 Beaufort *(13)*
8 Berkeley *(37)*
9 Calhoun *(5)*
10 Charleston *(32)*
11 Cherokee *(5)*
12 Chester *(6)*
13 Chesterfield *(5)*
14 Clarendon *(5)*
15 Colleton *(16)*
16 Darlington *(17)*
17 Dillon *(4)*
18 Dorchester *(21)*
19 Edgefield *(1)*
20 Fairfield *(7)*
21 Florence *(16)*
22 Georgetown *(32)*
23 Greenville *(25)*
24 Greenwood *(2)*
25 Hampton *(17)*
26 Horry *(27)*
27 Jasper *(16)*
28 Kershaw *(11)*
29 Lancaster *(8)*
30 Laurens *(5)*
31 Lee *(6)*
32 Lexington *(16)*
33 Marion *(4)*
34 Marlboro *(3)*
35 McCormick *(4)*
36 Newberry *(9)*
37 Oconee *(21)*
38 Orangeburg *(12)*
39 Pickens *(24)*
40 Richland *(17)*
41 Saluda *(5)*
42 Spartanburg *(10)*
43 Sumter *(12)*
44 Union *(6)*
45 Williamsburg *(14)*
46 York *(6)*

* Total number of different orchid species found in each county given in parenthesis.

Wild Orchids

Wild orchids have exerted an unnatural power over people for hundreds of years. In her bestselling book, *The Orchid Thief*, Susan Orleans quotes *The British Herbal Guide* of 1653, "They are hot and moist in operation, under the dominion of Venus, and provoke lust exceedingly."

What is the lure of these special plants? Initially, it may be their unique appearance. They grow in an almost infinite array of shapes and sizes. Some have compact flowers—many blooming on a stem at one time. Others have long curling and twisted lateral petals like something from a science fiction movie. And those fantastic lips—who could conceive of a plant that would be more outrageous than some of our native orchid species?

What could be more spectacular than the unusual assortment of colors and patterns present on each orchid flower?

What Is an Orchid?

One dictionary defines an orchid as "any of a large family (Orchidaceae) of plants of tropical and north temperate regions, bearing blossoms having two lateral petals similar, and a third [the lip] usually enlarged and often of grotesque shape." This is just a beginning. Much more can be said about this family of plants.

It is estimated that this family encompasses more than 30,000 species worldwide not including hybrids. Only about 153 species are native in North America (excluding Florida, which lists many species generally found much further south). South Carolina has approximately fifty-five native species (excluding natural hybrids). I use the word "approximately" since, even as I write this book, species designations are being reorganized, genera separated, combined, or otherwise reconfigured, making it difficult to state conclusively the absolute number of South Carolina's native orchid species.

Orchid flower characteristics likely make this family one of the most popular in the plant kingdom. The main parts of an orchid flower are as follows: (1) lip, (2) petals, (3) lateral sepals, (4) dorsal sepal, and (5) column. The following figures (not to scale) show examples of a few of the state's more common species with the prominent flower parts highlighted and numbered.

A major distinguishing orchid characteristic is the way that their pollen is distributed to pollinators. Most non-orchid species present their pollen by the pistil and stamen method. The pistil (part of the flower's female organ) is the

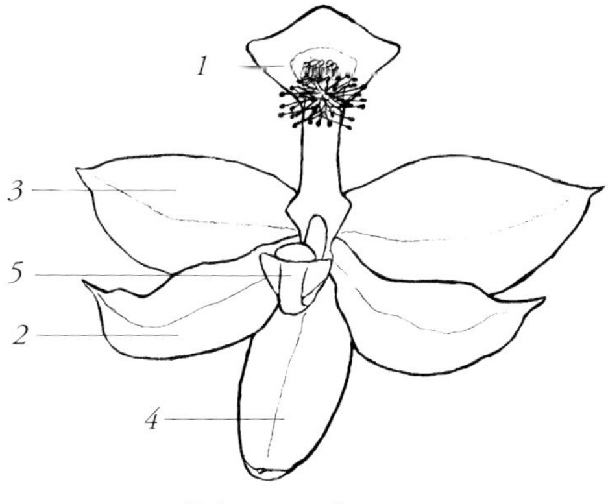

Calopogon tuberosus

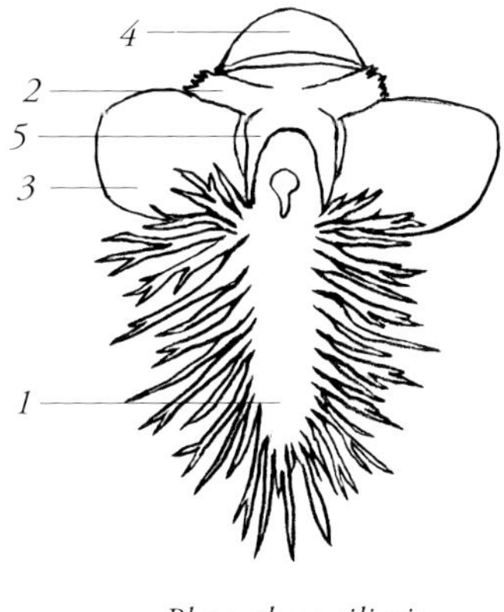

Platanthera ciliaris

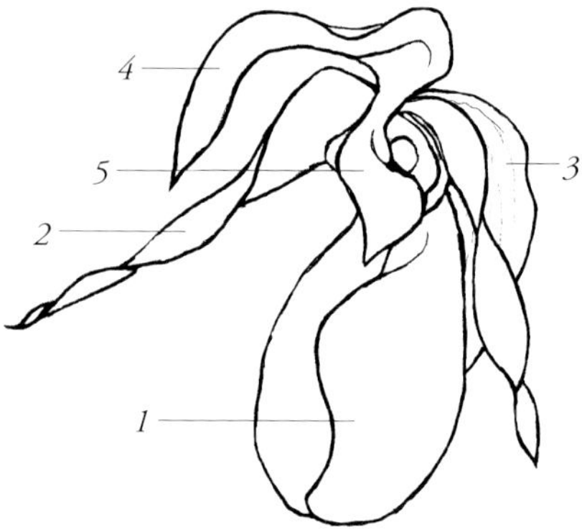

Cypripedium acaule

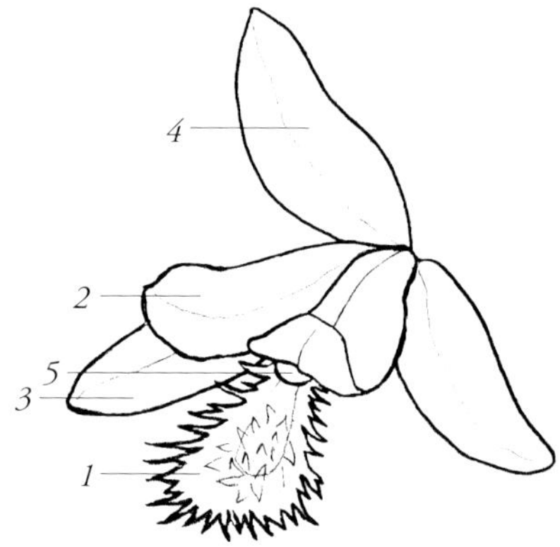

Pogonia ophioglossoides

part of the flower through which the pollen's sex cells travel to fertilize the eggs in the ovary. The style of the pistol is usually long and narrow, and the tip (stigma), to which the pollen adheres, produces a sticky substance. The stamens (part of the flower's male organs), which are usually grouped around the pistil, produce the dustlike pollen.

In orchids, the pistil and stamens are fused together in a structure called the column. Pollen is packaged in small detachable sacs or pods called pollinia (sing. pollinium). When the pollinator is retrieving or at least searching for nectar, the pollinium attaches to the pollinator by means of an exceedingly sticky substance and is carried to the next flower it visits. Once there, the pollinium adheres to the stigma. This pollination strategy is quite successful. But in the few orchid species that produce no nectar, pollination is dependent on naive insects who have not yet learned that there is no nectar reward for pollination.

Once the flower is fertilized successfully, seeds are produced. Many orchid species produce thousands to millions of seeds for each flower that is fertilized. These seeds are, in many cases, as small as dust particles and are carried off in the slightest breeze. By producing this prodigious amount of seeds, orchids insure that at least some seeds will fall in an area suitable for sustaining new life. With the proper nutrition, they will grow into viable plants.

In a strange relationship between living organisms, orchid plants are dependent on life-sustaining nutrients supplied by a specialized fungus. Since orchid seeds contain little or no nutritional supply for growth (endosperm), germination depends upon this relationship. In order for the seed to develop, it must be associated with this fungus.

Some orchid species are mycotropic and depend on certain fungi to help convert decaying organic matter to a usable food source. These particular orchid species do not produce chlorophyll and thus are unable to use sunlight to make food that is used for growth.

This relationship is very complex and is presently being studied in great depth. There are several select fungal species that form associations with orchids. It is this mycorrhizal relationship that explains why many native orchid species will not survive when transplanted—even if they are transplanted to an environment quite similar to that of their origin.

Because the fungal component of the mycorrhizae is exceedingly fragile and because many orchid species have quite delicate root systems, it is very important not to attempt to obtain orchid species from the wild except in situations of organized plant "rescue." These situations are usually a last-ditch effort to remove the plants from an imminent danger such as a road widening or a ground clearing. Even in situations such as these, where the most rigorous precautions are taken, a large percentage of the plants do not survive, and the ones that do survive usually fail to live for more than a year.

If you are determined to cultivate some of South Carolina's native orchid species, visit a nursery that specializes in native plants. Often, they will have certain species that have been "domesticated" and are more suited for the home garden. The best policy is to leave the wild plants in their native environment where they will live to bloom another day.

Wild Orchids
of South Carolina

Puttyroot Orchid
Adam-and-Eve Orchid

Aplectrum hyemale (Mühlenberg ex Willdenow) Nuttall

Genus: Aplectrum—From Greek, meaning "without spur," referring to the spurless nature of the flowers, which resemble those of the genus *Platanthera* (the spurred fringed orchids).

Species epithet: hyemale—From Latin, meaning "of winter," referring to the single solitary leaf that remains green throughout the winter.

Description: The three-by-ten-inch leaf that appears in fall to midwinter has many heavy, white, parallel veins. This leaf usually has withered when the eighteen-inch flower stalk appears in spring.

Each one-inch flower is generally a dull yellow or green with mahogany or purplish brown tips. A single stalk may contain as many as two dozen or as few as ten flowers. Several to many plants may appear in a single grouping, but not all plants will bloom in a single season.

In flower: Late April to early June.

Habitat: Rich, damp oak woods.

Range: It is reported from five upstate counties.

Pollinators: Frequently pollinated by bees and ants.

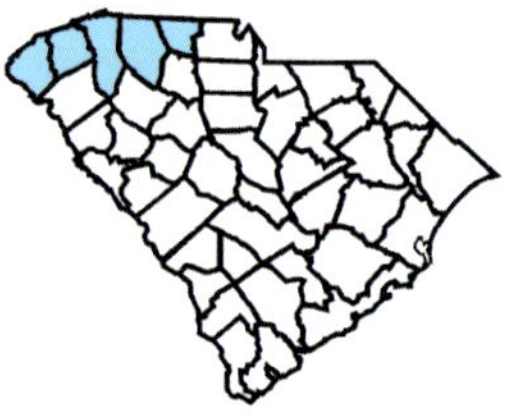

Take a casual stroll through the rich woods of the upstate's four most northwestern counties in January or February, and you will most likely see the peculiar, bloomless leaf of the puttyroot orchid—if you know what you are looking for.

The leaf is two to three inches wide and up to ten inches in length. It shows distinct parallel venation that is purplish in very young leaves and white in the mature leaves of late winter. It has the appearance of an unfolded accordion. The leaf usually, but not always, withers before the flower stalk presents itself around mid-May in South Carolina.

Winter leaf of the puttyroot orchid.

With careful observation, you can easily distinguish the leaf of the puttyroot orchid from the only other orchid found in South Carolina that has a single leaf in midwinter, the crane-fly orchid *(Tipularia discolor)*. The leaf of the puttyroot orchid is larger and more heavily veined and is usually blue green on both sides. The leaf of the crane-fly orchid is dull green on top and deep magenta purple on the underside and shows only a few very thin dark veins and wrinkles on the upperside of the leaf. When these plants are in bloom, the leaves of both orchids are usually brown and withered.

Due to the muted color of the puttyroot orchid, the blooming stalk is quite difficult to spot popping up in the sun-dappled leaf litter and low-growing vegetation that typically surrounds it. The flower is usually a muted yellow or green with a white lip. The petals and sepals may be tipped with a mahogany or purplish brown color. The stem is usually about sixteen to eighteen inches high and has anywhere from ten to twenty flowers. In late summer, the stem dries and produces seed capsules that may remain until the next flowering season.

The common name, puttyroot orchid, is derived from the puttylike substance found in the interior of the corm, or modified stem. Early settlers were thought to use this substance to mend broken pottery.

An alternate name, Adam-and-Eve, is derived from the nature of the plant's method of vegetative reproduction. Each year, the plant sprouts from a new corm. The previous year's corm remains attached, although withered. The new corm rises from the older one in the fashion of Eve rising from Adam's rib.

Stem of a puttyroot orchid with fifteen flowers. Two more blooming stems are in the background.

NOTES:

Bog Rose
Dragon's-mouth

Arethusa bulbosa Linnaeus

Genus: Arethusa—Named after a Greek nymph, Arethusa, who was turned into a river. Since this plant is found in very wet habitats, it is aptly named.

Species epithet: bulbosa—From Latin, referring to the corm, or swollen portion of the base of the stem, that is shaped like a bulb.

Description: This orchid has a single (rarely two) magenta (very rarely white or lilac blue) flower sitting on a four- to six-inch-tall stem. The one-inch petals and sepals generally point upward, while the lip curls downward like a tongue, hence the name dragon's-mouth. The lip is usually white or pink with deep purple markings. In the center of the lip is an area of yellow to orange protuberances resembling bristles of pollen. The solitary grasslike leaf, which clasps the stem, appears to be absent at flowering time but develops more fully later in the season.

In flower: Late May to early June.

Habitat: Rich, wet, meadows and sphagnous bogs.

Range: Rare. Reported from only two counties in the state. Due to the extremely fragile nature of its preferred environment and the ephemeral nature of the plants, this species may no longer be found in the state.

Pollinators: Since it offers little or no nectar, it is thought to be pollinated by inexperienced bumblebees, offering the promise of a meal, but giving no reward.

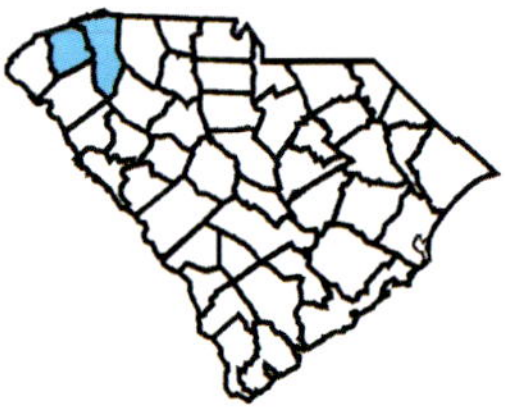

Finding a South Carolina orchid species that has only a historical record is an enormous task. *Arethusa bulbosa* has not been seen in its typical South Carolina habitats in many years. There are several reasons why these plants have disappeared. The primary one is habitat distruction or degradation. Habitats need not be paved over or filled in to destroy orchid populations. They can be drained or become so overgrown that fragile plants can no longer find suitable conditions to survive.

Back-to-back pair of Arethusa bulbosa *flowers.*

The sepals point up like little ears at attention, while the petals bend forward to protect the column and lip.

A few of South Carolina's mountain bogs and fens still remain, but they have been greatly reduced in size and in their abililty to support fragile species. Fortunately, an upstate bog that once supported *A. bulbosa* still provides a good home for another rare plant, *Helonias bullata,* or swamp pink.

In order to obtain photographs for this book, I traveled to one of the premier locations for this species—Maine. There, in late spring, wet meadows and bogs provide an ideal habitat for *A. bulbosa*. In some locales, these orchids, which are rare elsewhere, grow in profusion, sometimes appearing in groups of a dozen or more plants. Seeing this local abundance causes me to daydream of how some parts of South Carolina looked in the not too distant past.

Protecting areas that currently provide suitable habitat for our delicate orchid species is a job for all of us who regard the outdoors as a spiritual center for our lives. Attempting to save these plants for future generations is an undertaking worthy of each one of us.

Unusually large group of Arethusa bulbosa *growing in a secluded bog.*

NOTES:

Calopogon

The genus *Calopogon* is represented by five species within North America. One of these, *Calopogon oklahomensis*, was reportedly found in South Carolina, but no locations can currently be verified for this species, although historical records exists. *Calopogon oklahomensis* is a species of the open prairie, but occurrences of this type of environment have been so severely reduced in South Carolina, that there is little hope of finding it in the wild.

The remaining four species, *C. barbatus, C. multiflorus, C. pallidus,* and *C. tuberosus,* present such similar flowers that it warrants some discussion of how to distinguish between them in the field. These four species grow in similar environments, although they may bloom at different times during the year.

The first two reported species, *C. barbatus* and *C. multiflorus,* are found blooming during April and May. The flowers of both species are rather small—usually less than one inch wide. All of the flowers on a particular plant usually open within a day or so of each other. Considering these similarities, there are a few characteristics that one can use to distinguish between them in the field.

Calopogon multiflorus is almost completely dependent on prescribed burns to clear away competitive vegetation. Without the burns, *C. multiflorus* probably sends up seasonal leaves but fails to bloom.

When *C. multiflorus* does bloom, its five to fifteen flowers usually appear in an elongated arrangement along the stem, while the three to six flowers of *C. barbatus* are usually clustered at the top of the stem. The single most distinguishing characteristic, though, is the shape of the petals. The petal of *C. barbatus* is pandurate, or fiddle-shaped, while the petal of *C. multiflorus* is larger toward the distal (tip) portion than it is in the middle or proximal (lower) portion of the petal. (See the figure on the next page for comparison.)

The next two reported species, *C. pallidus* and *C. tuberosus,* usually bloom from May to July. The visual differences between these two species are more marked than the differences between *C. barbatus* and *C. multiflorus.* The position of the petals and the shape of the sepals are important for identification. The flowers of *C. pallidus* appear to be stretched in the vertical direction because the petals are curved forward while the lateral sepals are curved up and back. While the sepals of *C. tuberosus* are straight and point in opposite directions, the petals are curved slightly forward giving an overall triangular appearance to the flowers.

One other significant difference between these species is flower color. Although pale forms and even a white form of *C. tuberosus* occasionally are found, the predominant color is a rich magenta purple. Within a single population of *C. pallidus,* flower color is generally more richly varied, with pale colors and white predominating.

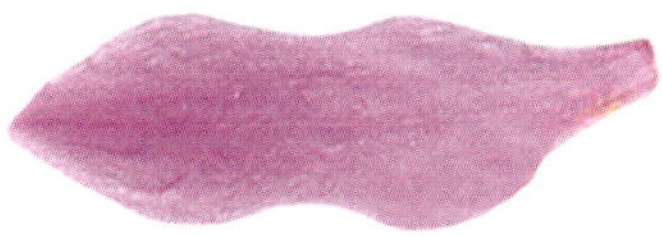

Calopogon barbatus

Calopogon multiflorus

Calopogon pallidus

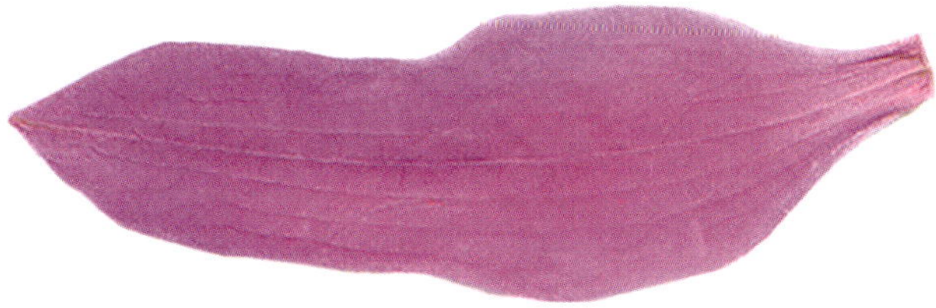

Calopogon tuberosus

Petal shapes of the state's four extant Calopogon *species. These are 4X photo enlargements of actual petals.*

Bearded Grass-pink

Calopogon barbatus (Walter) Ames

Genus: Calopogon—From two Greek words meaning "beautiful beard," referring to the stamen-like bristles or beard on the lip.

Species epithet: barbatus—From Latin, referring to the beard on the lip.

Description: This grass-pink is distinguished by a cluster of three to six pink flowers that all open at about the same time. Each flower is less than one inch across, sporting an upper (nonresupinate) lip with yellow or orange bristles and a curved and winged column projecting from the center of the flower. Another distinguishing feature is the pandurate (fiddle-shaped) shape of the petals that are widest below the middle. The slender stem sprouts from a base of erect, narrow, grasslike leaves.

In flower: April to May.

Habitat: Pinelands, meadows, and savannahs.

Range: Generally, only along the coast; however, it has been reported from Darlington County, as well.

Pollinators: The *Calopogon* species offer the lure of pollen to naive, recently emerged bees, but the offer is not fulfilled. The beard is only part of an ingenious deception. When an insect lands on the beard, the lip swings down, hingelike, placing the insect's head and back on the column thereby picking up the pollinium, or placing the pollinum on the stigma if the insect already carries a load on its back.

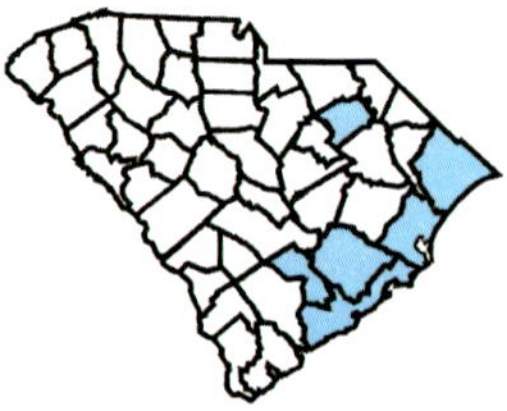

What a lovely little orchid is *Calopogon barbatus*. By little, I mean that the entire plant is seldom over six to eight inches tall, and the flowers are frequently less than one inch across. Each stem rises from a grasslike leaf that is only a couple of inches long and no more than one-eighth inch wide.

These small plants are very hard to see except when they are in full bloom. Even then, if the surrounding grasses and shrubby plants are dense, this orchid is often hidden. Many times, *C. barbatus* can be found growing under the shade of immature pines or even in the shadows of a number of different species of pitcher plants *(Sarracenia* spp.*)*. Both the *Calopogon* and the pitcher plants like their roots in damp soil.

Five Calopogon barbatus *plants blooming in a damp roadside ditch.*

When these orchids bloom, it is not unusual to find several color variations present. The typical color is a bright pink, tinged with a darker pinkish purple. Sometimes, very light pink or even bluish lilac-colored flowers are seen. When I look at a single flower, what usually stands out for me is the cluster of bright yellow bristles on the lip. They resemble stamens full of pollen, but the truth is they are faking it. This yellow "fuzz," or pseudopollen, is there only to lure an inexperienced bee to visit the flower, where it will hopefully perform the simple act of transferring the real pollinium to the stigma.

Lilac-colored group of Calopogon barbatus *flowers.*

NOTES:

Many-flowered Grass-pink

Calopogon multiflorus Lindley

Genus: Calopogon—From two Greek words meaning "beautiful beard," referring to the stamen-like bristles or beard on the lip.

Species epithet: multiflorus—From Latin, meaning "many-flowered," referring to the cluster of flowers on the stem.

Description: The bright magenta pink flowers of the many-flowered grass-pink are less than one inch in diameter and have a golden yellow crest of bristles on the lip. A distinguishing feature of the "rounded" flowers is the shape of the petals, which are widest above the middle. The bloom stem supports from five to fifteen flowers, most of which open at about the same time. The one or two leaves are slender and about four inches in length at maturity.

This species does best in environments that are subject to prescribed burns in late winter. It is known to bloom six to eight weeks after a burn, thriving due to lack of vegetative competition.

In flower: April to early May.

Habitat: Rather dry meadows and longleaf pine savannahs.

Range: Rare. Reported only from an area encompassing a small part of Berkeley County and Charleston County.

Pollinators: The *Calopogon* species offer the lure of pollen to naive, recently emerged bees, but the offer is not fulfilled. The beard is only part of an ingenious deception. When an insect lands on the beard, the lip swings down, hingelike, placing the insect's head and back on the column thereby picking up the pollinum, or placing the pollinum on the stigma if the insect already carries a load on its back.

The landscape is scorched and black. Shoots of spring greenery are just beginning to punch through the top layer of sandy soil. The picture is quite desolate, but this is the preferred habitat for one of South Carolina's rarest orchids, the many-flowered grass-pink. If it were not for periodic (annual) prescribed winter burns in the longleaf pine flatwoods, this rare orchid might not be found in any location in the southeast.

Notice the single, thin, vertical leaf at the base of the plant. This leaf will double in length as the plant matures.

This orchid hates competition. The fewer plants growing around it, the better. Quick ground fires that completely remove the past year's growth provide it the solitary setting it requires for its annual appearance.

After sprouting in early spring, a single leaf, sometimes two, appears clasping the bloom stem. There may be as many as fifteen flowers or as few as a single flower on a stem. Once the flower buds mature, they open in quick succession, sometimes taking only a couple of days for all of the flowers to open. They remain open for a couple of days, then wither and drop to the ground.

The arrangement of flowers appears elongated, so that when the inflorescence is in full bloom, its outline forms a narrow cylinder. The plant may be about six to sixteen inches tall, but it usually averages around eight to ten inches.

Flower color is usually a deep pinkish magenta, but pale magenta flowers

The tapering shape of the petals is a distinguishing feature of this species. It is widest past the middle of the petal.

can also be found. This is the only *Calopogon* that has a strong floral fragrance when in full anthesis. The other grass-pinks have either no fragrance or a very light citronella fragrance.

If one had to use a single distinguishing feature to differentiate this species from others in the genus *Calopogon*, it would be the shape of the petals. The petals of this species are wider on the outside (distal) half of the petal and gradually reduce in width toward the inner (proximal) point of attachment. The flowers appear to have a "rounded" profile due to the petals and the dorsal and lateral sepals having a similar length.

I find that this is the most desirable of the *Calopogon* species growing in the state. It will certainly be your good fortune to find one or more of these plants blooming in the early spring.

NOTES:

Pale Grass-pink

Calopogon pallidus (Chapman)

Genus: Calopogon—From two Greek words meaning "beautiful beard," referring to the stamen-like bristles or beard on the lip.

Species epithet: pallidus—From Latin, meaning "pale" or "pallid," referring to the color of the sepals and petals.

Description: The flower is often pale pink or white with a purplish marking on the lip and the tips of the petals. The one-inch flowers are arranged vertically on the stem and open in succession from the bottom to the top. A distinguishing feature is that the lateral sepals are curved back toward the stem while the petals are curved forward. Each flower sports an upper (non-resupinate) lip with yellow or orange bristles and a curved and winged column that projects from the center of the flower. The slender stem sprouts from a base of one or two narrow, vertical, grasslike leaves.

In flower: May to July.

Habitat: Open, damp pine stands, meadows, savannahs, marshes, and swamps.

Range: Generally along the coastal plain but also in the piedmont.

Pollinators: The *Calopogon* species offer the lure of pollen to naive, recently emerged bees, but the offer is not fulfilled. The beard is only part of an ingenious deception. When an insect lands on the beard, the lip swings down, hingelike, placing the insect's head and back on the column thereby picking up the pollinum, or placing the pollinum on the stigma if the insect already carries a load on its back.

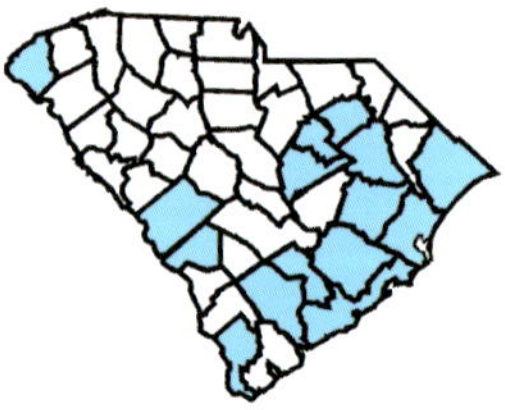

When looking at this orchid head-on, it is easy to see the lateral compression that distinguishes this species from the other orchids in the genus. This narrowing of perspective is due mainly to the lateral sepals being reflexed and curved in a backward direction.

Pink shades of Calopogon pallidus.

The stem supports several flowers and is quite thin and about a foot or more in height. Although several flowers may be open at any one time, the flowers open separately and sequentially from the bottom of the stem to the top.

The typical color for *Calopogon pallidus* is some shade of pink. Except in the case of the pure white-flowered form, there is generally a bit of deep pink or purple on the lip or tips of the sepals and petals. In addition, it is common to see a blossom with an overall dark pinkish cast on the petals and sepals.

Wind is an important factor when photographing this species. The thin stem and widely flared sepals act like a sail, trapping even the lightest movement of air and making photographing the flowers extremely difficult.

Sometimes, when I am lucky enough to find one or more of these beautiful orchids in flower, I am also presented with some of nature's critters, who also seem to like the view. The previous full-page picture demonstrates this serendipity. A cricket has made lunch of the bud directly above the open blossom. Fortunately for the photograph, it did not munch on the opened flower. Perhaps it was saving it for a later meal.

White forms of Calopogon pallidus *(clockwise from upper left): true white-flowered form with no pink or yellow, white form with yellow but no pink, white form with yellow and pink highlights.*

NOTES:

Common Grass-pink

Calopogon tuberosus (Linnaeus) Britton, Sterns, and Poggenberg

Genus: Calopogon—From two Greek words meaning "beautiful beard," referring to the stamen-like bristles or beard on the lip.

Species epithet: tuberosus—From Latin, meaning "tuberous," describing the bulblike corm.

Description: The flower color is a bright magenta, pinkish purple, lavender, or light pink and is rarely white. The one- to two-inch flowers are arranged vertically on the stem, opening in succession from the bottom to the top. There may be from four to twenty flowers on a stem. Each flower sports an upper (nonresupinate) lip with yellow or orange bristles and a curved and winged column projecting from the center of the flower. The slender stem sprouts from a base of narrow, grasslike leaves.

In flower: Mid-May to early July.

Habitat: Strongly acid conditions: bogs and wet, grassy meadows.

Range: Reported from the mountains, coastal plain, and other scattered locations in the state.

Pollinators: The *Calopogon* species offer the lure of pollen to naive, recently emerged bees, but the offer is not fulfilled. The beard is only part of an ingenious deception. When an insect lands on the beard, the lip swings down, hingelike, placing the insect's head and back on the column thereby picking up the pollinum, or placing the pollinum on the stigma if the insect already carries a load on its back.

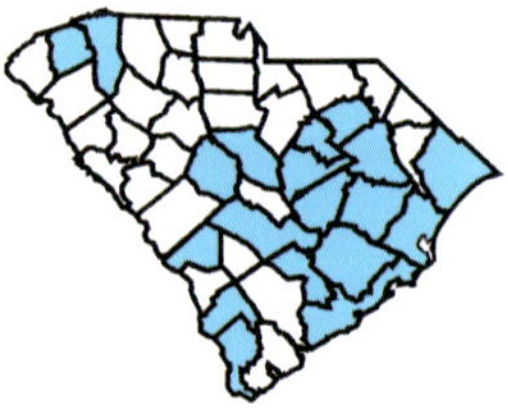

Coming across a clump of these beauties will surely open your eyes, as it did mine. Actually, this species is what piqued my interest in the state's native wild orchids. The first ones I saw were on the bank of a pond in a little-known heritage preserve in Greenville County. I would have overlooked them had I not left the path and wandered down to the edge of the pond to check for other blooming wildflowers.

To me, the most interesting thing about this species is the method it uses for pollination. First, the flower is nonresupinate. That means, unlike most other orchid species, its flowers are "upside down." The lip is the uppermost petal on the flower. The flowers of most of the state's other orchids begin this way in bud, but as the flower opens, it turns "right-side up."

Pale pink form of Calopogon tuberosus *(left) and white form (right).*

This upside down approach has its advantages. When a bee lands on the bearded portion of the lip, expecting to find nectar or at least pollen, the lip swings down on a natural hinge placing the back of the insect directly on the pollen receptor, or column.

If the bee has recently visited another *Calopogon tuberosus* flower, it may be carrying a pollen sac (pollinium) on its back. The pollinium will adhere to the top of the column where it will pollinate the flower. The hinge approach to pollination works very well for this species. Most of the flowers I have seen later will have fertile seed pods.

These two flowering stems of grass-pink would seem to be at home even in a tropical setting. Note the flower in the lower left corner. It has been visited by an insect that triggered its natural hinge mechanism.

If the interesting nature of this species' method of pollination does not capture your attention, then surely the lively variation of color and the two dozen flowers on each stem will. Unlike some of the other orchid species in the state, this one really does show most of the characteristics that people associate with tropical orchids.

The pictures included in this chapter show just a few of the many color variations of *C. tuberosus*. I have seen much darker magenta flowers as well as lighter pink and white ones. Some of the paler flowers may even have streaks or spots of pink or magenta. Local environmental conditions may play a role in determining the color.

NOTES:

Smaller Rosebud Orchid
Upland Spreading Pogonia

Cleistes bifaria (Fernald) Catling and Gregg

Genus: *Cleistes*—From Greek, meaning "closed," referring to the tubular shape of the flowers, which are open only at one end.

Species epithet: *bifaria*—From Latin, referring to the "two places" where they are found—the coast and the mountains.

Description: The single, tubular flower is generally about one to two inches long and is supported on a stem that has a solitary leaf about half way up the stem and a single leaf bract at the base of the ovary. The narrow, mahogany-colored sepals stretch upward and are about the same length as the petals. The front-facing petals that form the tube are either white or light pink. The lip protrudes beyond the petals and has purple veins and markings. It also sports a curved center section containing a blotch of yellow bristles.

Besides the length of the flower, a characteristic that distinguishes this species from *Cleistes divaricata* is a broad, lance-shaped leaf and bract.

In flower: May to July.

Habitat: Swamps and wet boggy areas.

Range: Reported only from two upstate counties, one central county, and along the coastal plain.

Pollinators: Bumblebees.

Currently, *C. bifaria* is being studied closely, possibly leading to a future differentiation between the mountain and coastal plain populations (Smith et al. 2004).

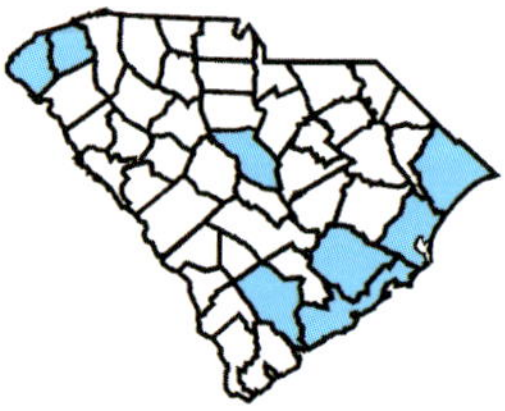

Our photography group had just entered the longleaf pine savannah looking for the rather elusive smaller rosebud orchid *(Cleistes bifaria)*. These plants do not grow in large groups, nor do they grow high above the surrounding vegetation. Finding them requires wading through the ferns and wire grass that make up the ground cover of many of South Carolina's savannahs.

On this trip, I spotted my first plant about ten feet away from a group of pitcher plants that had caught my eye. It was just barely visible, nestled in the wire grass. Its white petals glowed in the morning sun. The leaves and sepals blended well with the surrounding vegetation, making it otherwise difficult to spot.

Notice the tight curls in both the sepals and the tips of the petals of this flower.

Looking at the blossom up close, it is easy to see why many consider this species as the state's most beautiful native orchid. The lip is heavily veined and has rich magenta, reddish purple, and yellow coloring. This contrasts with the bright white petals and bright green leaves. If you gently nudge apart the petals, you can see the short column that houses the reproductive parts of the flower.

This species differs from its cousin, the rosebud orchid, *Cleistes divaricata*, in several respects. The most pronounced is the color of the petals. Although the petals of the smaller rosebud orchid are usually a bright white, some can be found with a slightly pinkish cast, but never as deep pink as the rosebud orchid. Another distinguishing feature is the leafy floral bract just behind the flower. It is generally shorter, blunter, and broader in the smaller rosebud orchid. Of course, some plants may be found that exhibit, for one reason or another, a narrower floral bract.

These photographs are from coastal plains populations.

This orchid is sought after by many orchid enthusiasts. It is easy to see why many consider this species as being our most beautiful.

NOTES:

Rosebud Orchid
Spreading Pogonia

Cleistes divaricata (Linnaeus) Ames

Genus: Cleistes—From Greek, meaning "closed," referring to the tubular shape of the flowers, open only at the end.

Species epithet: divaricata—From Latin, referring to the "widely spreading" nature of the sepals.

Description: The single, tubular flower is generally about two inches or more in length and is supported on a stem that has a solitary leaf about half way up the stem and a single, pointed floral bract at the base of the ovary. The narrow, mahogany-colored sepals stretch upward and are about the same length as the petals. The front-facing petals that form the tube are usually some shade of pink. The lip protrudes beyond the petals and has purple veins and markings. It also sports a curved center section sometimes containing a blotch of yellow bristles. A single stem with two flowers is quite rare.

Besides the length of the flower, a characteristic that distinguishes this species from *Cleistes bifaria* is a narrow, lance-shaped floral bract.

In flower: May to July.

Habitat: Swamps, savannahs, woods, and meadows.

Range: Generally along the inner coastal plain.

Pollinators: Bumblebees.

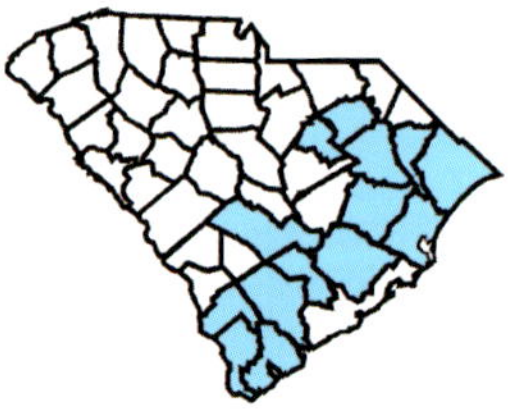

Unlike its relative, the smaller rosebud orchid *(Cleistes bifaria),* the rosebud orchid is generally taller and usually pokes it head above the surrounding vegetation. This makes it a bit easier to see among the wire grass and ferns of the savannah. It sometimes reaches a foot or more in height and has a flower that is two or more inches long.

The petals are usually a delicate shade of magenta pink and complement the dark mahogany purple sepals that flare out behind the flower. Besides the color of the petals, the shape of the floral bract helps distinguish this species from the smaller rosebud orchid. It is usually long, narrow, and pointed.

The curl in the petal tips adds a dainty and delicate quality to the blossom.

In some savannahs, the rosebud orchid is the dominant orchid species, while in others, the smaller rosebud orchid dominates. However, it is not unusual to find them both growing side by side, making it quite easy to contrast the distinguishing features.

In a good year, the savannah is literally dotted with pink blossoms nodding in the gentle breezes that continuously sweep over the grasses and ferns.

Often, several different *Calopogon* species, such as *C. pallidus* or *C. tuberosus,* are found growing in association with rosebud orchids. If you are lucky, you might also spot a few species of *Spiranthes,* as well.

If I could wish for one thing, it would be to find a large clump of rosebud orchids in full bloom. I imagine that this would be a spectacular sight. The best I have found so far is two plants blooming about three inches apart. It appears to prefer a relatively solitary existence.

The next time you find yourself along the coastal plain in a longleaf pine savannah during the spring or early summer, be on the lookout for this beautiful orchid. You will definitely be surprised and pleased with its delicate beauty.

The long petals cover the reproductive parts underneath but curl back to expose the heavily veined lip, which is used as a landing pad for visiting insects.

NOTES:

Spotted Coralroot Orchid

Corallorhiza maculata (Rafinesque) Rafinesque

Genus: Corallorhiza—From two Greek words meaning "coral rhizome," with coral referring to the twisted coral-like growth of the rhizome.

Species epithet: maculata—From Latin, meaning "spotted."

Description: This is a saprophytic species that commonly is found over much of the northern portion of the United States. South Carolina is probably its southernmost distribution, at least in the eastern United States.

A thick stem, six to eighteen inches tall, rises from a knobby, tuberous root, which is multiply branched and is the source of the name "coralroot." It frequently occurs in large groups scattered over the forest floor. It begins blooming in late spring and continues through the summer.

The flower consists of petals and sepals that closely match the tan or flesh color of the stem. The color of the sepals tends to be a darker purplish pink toward the tips and outer edges. The lip is enlarged and is basically white with several deep reddish purple spots. The lip is rarely white and without any spots. This species does not produce leaves.

In flower: Late June to September.

Habitat: Shady, mature deciduous woods.

Range: Reported from only Pickens County and Hampton County.

Pollinators: Insects, possibly.

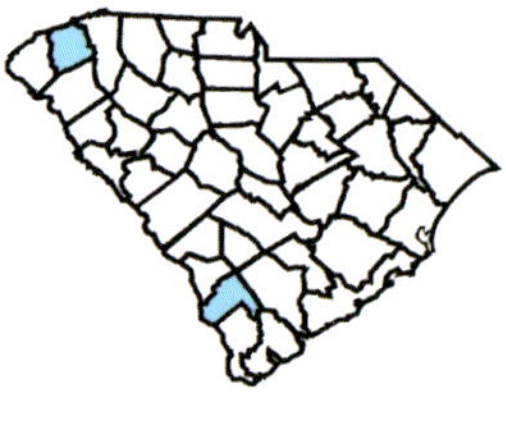

Although *Corallorhiza maculata* has been reported only from two counties in the state, chances are good that it might be found in other locations. The state's northern counties are particularly rich in damp hickory and oak woods, its favorite habitat. It begins blooming in late July.

Two plants in full bloom and one just getting started.

Being a saprophyte, it is capable of surviving without chlorophyll. Since it contains no chlorophyll, it therefore cannot use sunlight to make food. An underground supply of rotting vegetation provides it with the necessary nutrition for survival. In any case, it seems to be a happy relationship, since these plants return year after year putting on quite a beautiful display.

Actually, this species is fairly difficult to spot in the shadowy leaf litter of the forest. It is much easier to find them by squatting down and surveying the general area where these plants are supposed to be growing.

The flowers are quite colorful, but a magnifier is needed to appreciate them. The lip is white and usually shows several reddish purple spots. Sometimes, there is just a single large spot contrasting against the white background. The sepals are tan to flesh-colored and tend to a dark reddish brown on the tips.

The blooming period is quite lengthy, with some plants just sprouting as others close by are already going to seed. The seed is formed shortly after the flower is pollinated. When this happens, the

Close-up showing colorful lip and sepals.

flower droops and the ovary begins to swell. This is clearly illustrated in the picture on the opposite page. Notice the lower flowers on the blooming stems.

The day these plants were photographed, it was pouring rain, but being under the dense foliage of the oak forest, I hardly noticed. I'll use any excuse to get out into the field to photograph these beautiful creations, and a little rain never stops me.

NOTES:

Autumn Coralroot Orchid

Corallorhiza odontorhiza (Willdenow) Poiret

Genus: Corallorhiza—From two Greek words meaning "coral rhizome," with coral referring to the twisted coral-like growth of the rhizome.

Species epithet: odontorhiza—From two Greek words meaning "toothed rhizome." Many of the rhizomes exhibit a toothlike projection.

Description: This saprophytic orchid is unusual because it has two types of flowers: "cleistogamous" flowers that do not open and are self-pollinating, and "chasmogamous" flowers that open normally and are pollinated by insects. Each population of plants will have only one type of flower.

The ovaries of cleistogamous flowers appear swollen even as the flowers begin to mature. Those that do open fully exhibit a purple-spotted white lip while all of the other flower parts are a greenish purple. The thin stalk usually supports about twelve tiny flowers. This orchid can be found growing in large clusters. This species does not produce leaves.

In flower: Mid-August through October.

Habitat: Mixed forest conditions, including hardwood, hemlock, and pine.

Range: Scattered locations throughout the state, but less frequent on the coastal plain.

Pollinators: Cleistogamous form, self-pollinated; chasmogamous form, possibly pollinated by insects.

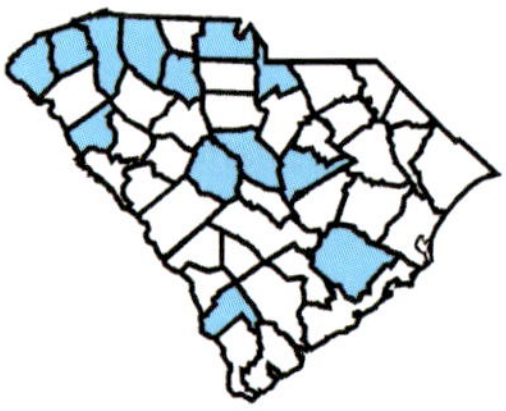

There they were at the end of a path that bordered the mountain stream—dozens of *Corallorhiza odontorhiza* in full bloom, poking through the abundant leaf litter. Each stem sported from eight to fifteen odd-looking flowers. This orchid will never win a beauty contest, but it is very interesting.

If you look closely, you can see the white lip under the "hood," which is formed by the dorsal sepal and petals.

I soon realized that the group of plants I was photographing were cleistogamous. This means that the flowers will never fully open. The internal reproductive parts are in immediate proximity to each other, thereby forcing self-pollination. This species also can produce chasmogamous flowers, which require an external agent, such as an insect, for pollination.

Since the flowers at my feet were cleistogamous, they were forming seeds even as the plant emerged from the forest floor. The ovaries were already swelling and drooping.

With magnification, you can see the tiny white lip under the "hood," which is formed by the dorsal sepal and the petals. Like some of the other *Corallorhiza* species, the white lip also has dark purple spots.

On cleistogamous plants, you will have to look under the flower to see the lip. On chasmogamous species, the lip is quite distinct and showy as is seen in *C. maculata.*

This species is also a saprophyte, which means that it obtains its nourishment from decaying matter

Note the swelling ovaries already forming seeds as the plant blooms.

under the soil's surface. It cannot make its own food via photosynthesis, but uses the services provided by certain fungi living in the soil. For this reason, these orchids are virtually impossible to transplant to the home garden.

Whenever I see this species in bloom, it reminds me that autumn is just around the corner, hastening another group of late-blooming orchids *(Spiranthes)* that will last until first frost.

NOTES:

Wister's Coralroot Orchid
Spring Coralroot Orchid

Corallorhiza wisteriana (Conrad)

Genus: Corallorhiza—From two Greek words meaning "coral rhizome," with coral referring to the twisted coral-like growth of the rhizome.

Species epithet: wisteriana—Named for the botanist Charles J. Wister (1782–1865) who first collected the plant in 1828.

Description: The tiny petals, sepals, and stem of this saprophytic species can be light brown or dark reddish brown. Occasionally, flowers with yellow green petals and sepals and pure white lips with pale purple spots can be found. Each thin stem has from four to ten flowers. The lip of the flower is usually white with magenta purple spots. A single population of these orchids can contain many blooming stems one year and only a few or even none the next year.

The rhizome that produces the blooming stems branches continuously with offshoots positioned at a sixty-degree angle. This gives the effect of branching coral. This species does not produce leaves.

In flower: Late March through May.

Habitat: Rocky calcareous soils and along creek banks.

Range: Thinly scattered in the mountains, piedmont, and coastal plain.

Pollinators: Possibly by small insects.

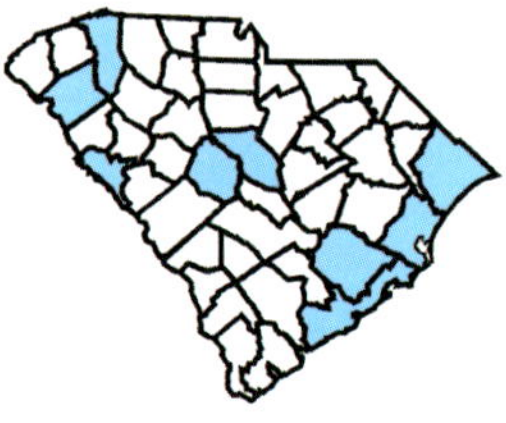

The calendar may say that it is almost spring, but the crunch of dead leaves underfoot and the palpable nip in the air suggest otherwise. This is the first of the state's orchids to bloom in the calendar year. Oddly enough, these plants seem to be able to survive some freezing nights without noticeable harm. If a plant wants to be the first to bloom and set its seeds, then that is a risk that it must take.

Close-up showing magenta purple spots on the lips. These spots may be pale purple on flowers whose sepals and petals are yellow green.

Scattered under the oak and pine trees in the woods are single stems and groups of stems each containing up to ten small flowers. When you finally spot this plant on the forest floor, what you see first are the white lips of its flowers because the remainder of the flower parts and the stem are the same color as the dead leaves and pine straw that litter the ground. Actually, the lips resemble little tongues hanging from each open flower.

The lip is bright white and, in most cases, is dotted with vivid magenta purple spots. In some rare cases, the lip is pure white with pale purple spots, and the petals, sepals, and stem are a curious yellow green.

Most of the stems that comprise rather large groups come from a single, branching rhizome. This rhizome branches in such a manner that it takes on the appearance of a branching coral, hence the name coralroot.

Photographing this species takes a great deal of patience, especially if you wish to use natural light to highlight the flowers. When I photographed the plants pictured in this chapter, I found myself running from plant to plant as the dappled light quickly shifted over the forest floor. Every couple of minutes, the light would filter through the bare limbs and twigs above, suddenly lighting up a particular stem or group of stems in perfect fashion. I always hope to get the ultimate photograph, and I could have stayed in that spot for hours waiting for that opportunity, but the pleasure of just walking around and enjoying the orchids growing around me won out in the end.

A clump of Wister's coralroot with almost two dozen blooming stems, most of them coming from a single, large underground rhizome.

NOTES:

Pink Lady's-slipper Orchid

Cypripedium acaule Aiton

Genus: *Cypripedium*—From the Greek "Cypris," describing an alternate name for the goddess Venus, and the Greek "pedis," describing the foot- or shoelike nature of its lip or pouch.

Species epithet: *acaule*—From Latin, meaning "without stem" referring to the leaves and flower stalk, which arise stemless from the rhizome.

Description: Each plant has two parallel-veined, downy, leathery leaves from which the flower stalk arises. The "inflated" lip of this orchid can be dark magenta pink, medium to light pink, or, very rarely, pure white. The two narrow petals and the sepals are usually a dark greenish to reddish brown. In the white-flowered form, the petals and sepals are yellow green.

The lip has a small vertical slit in the front through which insects enter during pollination. To exit, the insect must brush against the column at the base of the lip, which contains the pollinia, thus arming it for a visit to the next flower. This species may be found in large groups or just one or two plants on the forest floor.

In flower: Mid-April to mid-June.

Habitat: Usually in dry, oak-pine woods.

Range: Generally in the upstate and piedmont, but it has also been reported from Georgetown County.

Pollinators: Bees; since there is no nectar reward, likely inexperienced ones.

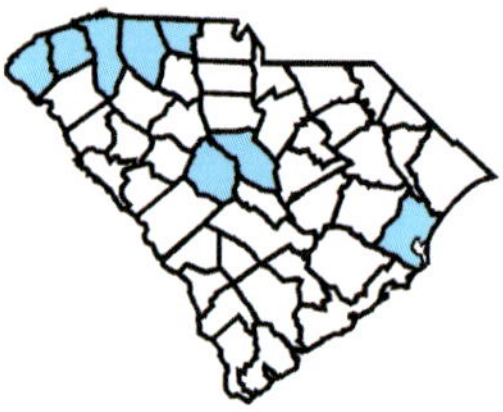

When you come across this orchid, especially in the upstate, you might see it covering large areas of the forest floor. Individual clumps of six to eight plants can be found, but more often, single plants or multiples of two or three plants are scattered over a large area.

Pink lady's-slipper orchids prefer the shaded understory of oak-pine woods. In fact, when I look for this orchid, I search out areas that have a predominant growth of white pine *(Pinus strobus)* or Virginia pine *(P. virginiana),* and usually I am rewarded with a fine show of orchid plants.

Though this orchid can be found in decent-sized clumps, not all of the plants will flower every year. In fact, less than 10 percent of plants in a particular area might be in flower during the bloom season. But, when you do find many plants in flower, it is quite a pretty sight.

The color variation of the pouchlike lip is quite remarkable, even within a single grouping of plants. The colors range from a pure white to a deep purplish rose. Other variation is found in the venation of the lip. Sometimes, the lip has a uniform color with just a slight blending of lighter to darker rose or pink. Other times, the lip may be strikingly veined showing a great deal of contrast between the colors.

Note the heavily veined lip on this pink lady's-slipper orchid.

An interesting feature of this orchid is its method of pollination. There is a narrow slit in the front center of the lip. The insect (usually a bee) must force itself into this slit in order to enter the lip. Once it is inside, the only exit is through the top portion of the lip. This requires that the insect brush against the pollen sacs on the column on its way out. The pollen sacs immediately attach to the back of the bee and are ready to be transported to the next flower.

This is an orchid that is fairly plentiful in the upstate. To find a population of pink lady's-slipper orchids, just wait until early May. Locate a stand of mature pine trees and take a few minutes to look around. There is a very good chance that you will find this orchid in bloom in the dappled shade of the pine boughs.

Showy group of pink lady's-slipper orchids spread out on the forest floor.

NOTES:

Large Yellow Lady's-slipper Orchid

Cypripedium parviflorum
Salisbury var. *pubescens* (Willdenow) Knight

Genus: *Cypripedium*—From the Greek "Cypris," describing an alternate name for the goddess Venus, and the word "pedis," describing the foot- or shoelike nature of its lip or pouch.

Species epithet: *parviflorum* var. *pubescens*—From Latin words meaning "small-flowered" and "downy."

Description: Each plant bears three to five well-developed leaves. The "inflated" lip of this orchid is bright yellow. The two narrow petals, as well as the sepals, are green at the base and are a slight reddish brown along the edges and toward the tip. The one- to two-inch pouch contains a small oval opening at the top where the base joins the stem. Insects enter through this opening during pollination. All parts of the flower except the lip are covered with fine downy hairs. The stem usually supports only one, sometimes two, flowers. This orchid may be found in rather large showy groups.

In flower: Late April through May.

Habitat: Moist wooded slopes and around bogs and swamps.

Range: Found in only five of the state's northern counties. There are two additional varieties, *C. parviflorum* var. *parviflorum* and *C. parviflorum* var. *makasin*, both of which occur outside of South Carolina.

Pollinators: Bees; since there is no nectar reward, likely inexperienced ones.

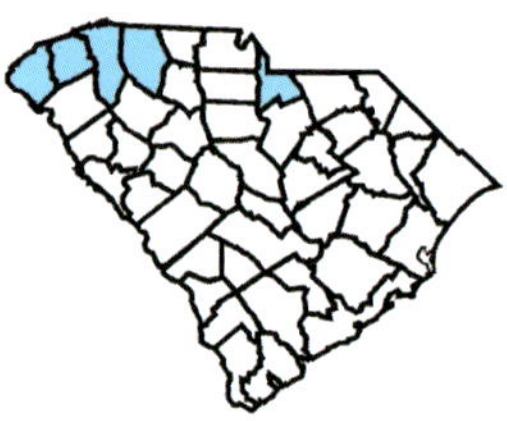

This is, without doubt, one of the state's showiest lady's-slipper orchids. Its large yellow flowers with purplish green sepals are easy to spot in the early spring against the fallen forest leaves. Before it flowers, the easiest way to spot this plant is by the bright yellow green foliage of its broad, veined leaves. It stands out against any neighboring grasses and shrubby plants that might be close by.

This species has had several name changes in recent years. For many decades, it was assigned the name *Cypripedium calceolus*, but that species is found strictly in Europe. Later, the name *Cypripedium parviflorum* var. *pubescens* was assigned. Sometimes name changes are difficult to keep up with, but it's all for

Large yellow lady's-slipper orchid a week or so before coming into full bloom.

the best. Distinguishing between species is important, and the use of a unique botanical name is one sure method to accomplish this.

Unfortunately, the flower of this plant is so well-known and so handsome that it is likely to be dug up from its home in the woods. The misguided soul who wishes to transplant this wild plant into the home garden doesn't realize that it has little chance of surviving for more than a year. The special fungus that it needs to supply nutrition through the roots will likely not survive the transplant, and the plant will die after it depletes its stored energy.

A safer approach for growing this orchid at home is to purchase domesticated plants at a nursery that specializes in nursery-grown orchids. In this way, the wild orchid remains in its intended place for all to see and the gardener has a viable plant to admire at home.

The same large yellow lady's-slipper flower exactly one week later.

NOTES:

Green-fly Orchid

Epidendrum magnoliae Mühlenberg

Genus: Epidendrum—From Greek, meaning "on tree," referring to its natural epiphytic habit of growing on tree trunks and branches.

Species epithet: magnoliae—From Latin, referring to "magnolia," the tree on which the type specimen was found growing.

Description: This orchid is found growing on trees or rocks. It is epiphytic not parasitic; it receives structural support only, not nourishment, from its host. It is a frost-tolerant plant usually found growing on tree limbs in association with resurrection fern. The dark, evergreen, leathery leaves are one to four inches long and about one-half inch wide. Its one-inch flowers are usually some shade of green or yellow green with touches of purplish green on the tips of the petals. Clusters of up to a dozen flowers may be found on each floral stem.

In flower: Late June through September.

Habitat: It is usually found growing in association with resurrection ferns on the limbs of swamp tupelo, live oak, southern magnolia, and bald cypress in the immediate vicinity of streams and rivers.

Range: Reported generally from counties in the outer coastal plain.

Pollinators: Bees.

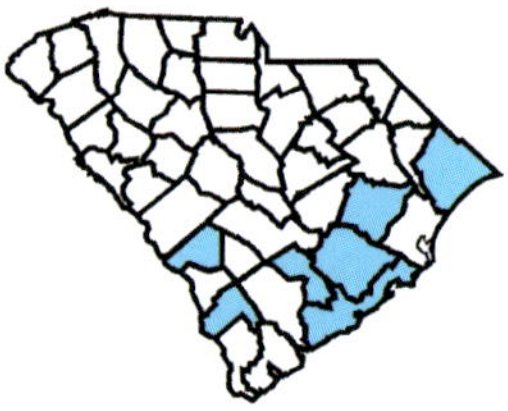

The heavy, humid air permeates the interior of the Francis Beidler Forest in the Four Holes Swamp area of the lowcountry, which is the ideal setting for our only epiphytic orchid, the green-fly orchid. Since constant humidity is required, you most likely will find this orchid perched on the trunk or limb of a tree that is standing in or hanging over water.

Green-fly orchid living on the branch of a live oak tree (Quercus virginiana).

There are several species of trees that fit this description: live oak *(Quercus virginiana)*, swamp tupelo *(Nyssa aquatica)*, southern magnolia *(Magnolia grandiflora),* and bald cypress *(Taxodium distichium)* to name a few. Although it grows directly on the bark of these trees, it is not a parasite—it uses the bark only as a foothold. Sometimes, the orchid plant is hidden by resurrection fern *(Polypodium polypodioides),* which prefers the same growing conditions and often shares the same neighborhood.

If you want to spot a group of these plants in the wild, look up, which is pretty hard to do when you are knee-deep in swamp muck fighting mosquitos and looking out for snakes and alligators. Many times the plants grow very high in the uppermost tree branches. The group pictured above was just above eye level on one of the large branches of a tree that had fallen in a storm; otherwise, I would have had to climb thirty or more feet to photograph it.

The southernmost coastline river systems of North Carolina form the northern limit of this beautiful orchid species. We are lucky to have it grace most of

Delicate, insect-like flowers of the green-fly orchid.

South Carolina's coastal river systems. Perhaps one day you will find yourself in this interesting habitat and eye-to-eye with these lovely flowers.

This orchid was previously known as *Epidendrum conopseum,* the species epithet denoting the *Conopsia* or green fly—hence the name green-fly orchid.

NOTES:

Showy Orchis

Galearis spectabilis (Linnaeus) Rafinesque

Genus: Galearis—From Latin, meaning "helmeted," referring to the shape of the connivent petals and dorsal sepal.

Species epithet: spectabilis—From Latin, meaning "notable" or "remarkable (showy)."

Description: The stalk has two to ten fragrant, bicolored flowers and rises from two broad, glossy leaves at its base. The entire plant is only about six inches tall, so its diminutive size helps hide it on the leafy forest floor.

The lip, to which is connected a tubular spur, is usually white, but it is not unusual to see it tinted by shades of pink. The dorsal sepal and petals converge to make up the "helmet," which is usually a shade of purple. Entirely white and entirely purple flowers have been reported.

In flower: April to July.

Habitat: Rich, open hardwood forests, moist slopes, and stream banks.

Range: Reported only from the four most northwest counties in the state.

Pollinators: Bumblebees.

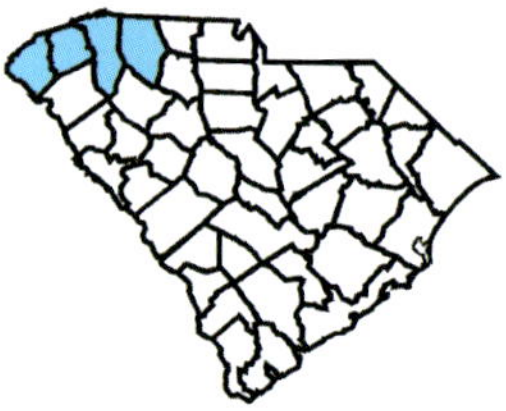

This dainty little orchid is a sight to behold when in full bloom. It may reach six inches at its greatest height, but more often, it is much shorter. When it grows intermingled with trillium, for example, it may not reach the underside of the trillium's large spreading leaves, and can be easily overlooked. In fact, I usually have to search an area closely before I spot one or more in flower.

Group of three showy orchis plants blooming simultaneously.

Showy orchis can form beds of twenty or more plants, but generally, the plants are scattered or are in groups of six or less. They almost always have just two shiny, oval leaves, but occasionally, you may spot a plant with a third leaf. The single stem sports as many as nine or ten flowers or as few as two.

This is another one of the spurred orchids, and its spur is easily seen upon close inspection. The flower is very fragrant—both spicy and sweet at the same time. Often you can smell its fragrance before you spot the flowers.

The color of the petals is quite variable. The helmet can be deep magenta purple, light lavender, or even white. The lip which is usually bright white, may also show streaks or blushes of pink or light purple.

I have seen this orchid bloom in full sun, but this is rare. It prefers to grow under overhanging tree limbs. Only on occasion does it peek out and catch the briefest rays of the sun.

Not all of the flowers show striking color differences. This one, for example, shows a light lavender helmet and a slightly pinkish lip.

NOTES:

Downy Rattlesnake Plantain

Goodyera pubescens (Wildenow) R. Brown

Genus: Goodyera—Named for the seventeenth-century English botanist John Goodyer.

Species epithet: pubescens—From Latin, meaning "hairy," referring to the fine hairs that cover almost every part of the plant.

Description: The entire plant is covered with fine hairs, though the petals, including the lip, are much less so. In this species, the evergreen leaf is heavily marked with whitish green veins and a wide, whitish midvein. The triangular spike of flowers is tightly packed on the top third of the stem. The flowers are small and rounded and have a waxy texture. The lip is pouchlike with the tip shaped into a short, rounded beak or spout.

This species frequently forms large beds, containing dozens of plants.

In flower: Mid-July through August.

Habitat: Dry oak-pine woods to damp hemlock woods and rhododendron thickets.

Range: It occurs in about two-thirds of South Carolina's counties, most notably in the mountains and piedmont, but can be found occasionally in the coastal plain.

Pollinators: Small bees.

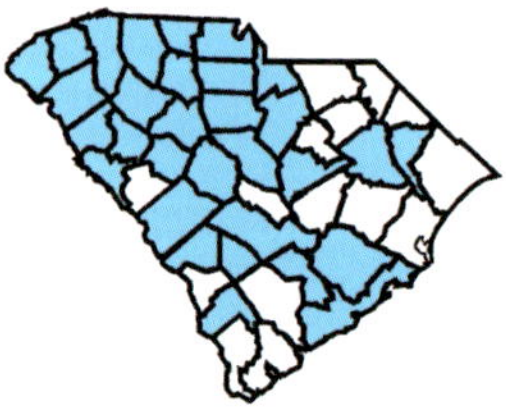

Each time I walk into the woods, especially in the upstate, I am on the lookout for the handsome leaves of the downy rattlesnake plantain. Its evergreen leaves are easy to spot in midwinter. They have a delicate network of white veins. A wide, white midvein runs down the center of each leaf making it stand out against the downy, soft, blue green background.

Rosette of veined, evergreen leaves (photo taken in early March).

It is not unusual to find very large beds of this orchid with its leafy rosettes popping up through the forest's leaf litter. The plant reproduces by underground runners and by seeds. Frequently, the dried seed-bearing stalks remain on the plants until just before the next blooming season.

The flowers are tiny and rounded. Upon close observation, they can appear quite amusing—like tiny white birds with their beaks open, ready to be fed. Each foot-tall blooming stalk can have as many as a hundred flowers. Almost all of the plant's parts, including the flowers, are covered with fine, downy hair, which is the origin of its common name.

This orchid is quite common in South Carolina, having been reported from about two-thirds of the state's counties. I suspect that with diligent searching, one could find it in all forty-six counties. Seeing a large group of these prolific orchids thrusting their torchlike inflorescences skyward is definitely a treat you will remember.

Cluster of downy rattlesnake plantains in flower.

NOTES:

Club-spur Orchid
Woodland Orchid

Gymnadeniopsis clavellata (Michaux) Luer

Genus: Gymnadeniopsis—From several Greek words, referring to similarity ("-opsis") to the genus *Gymnadenia*, orchids that have a naked ("gymn") gland ("aden"), meaning the viscidia are free or uncovered.

Species epithet: clavellata—From Latin "clavellatus," meaning "club-shaped," referring to the enlarged tip of the spur on each flower.

Description: This orchid generally has a single clasping leaf at its base and another about one-third the way up the stem. The leaf is six to eight inches in length and about one inch wide. The stem is about eight to twelve inches tall and sports a loose cluster of up to a dozen simple, greenish white or greenish yellow flowers at the top.

The lip of each quarter-inch flower is slightly larger at the end of the three-lobed tip. Each flower has a half-inch spur that points back and downward. The spur is enlarged at the end and shaped like a club, thus the name club-spur orchid.

In flower: June to September.

Habitat: Moist woods, bogs, stream banks, and meadows.

Range: Much of the state, from the mountains to the coastal plain.

Pollinators: Self-pollinating, although various insects may pay a visit.

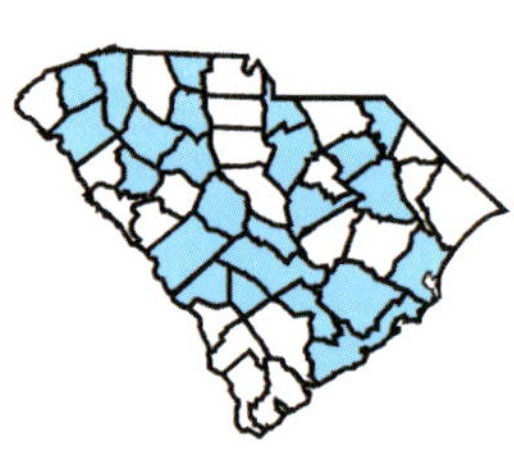

This little orchid is fairly common throughout the state. If you happen to look down at the right time and place, these small bright clusters of flowers will catch your eye. Although fairly well hidden among grasses and other small woodland plants, their shape and their occurrence in large groups helps with identification.

In the mountains, they begin to bloom about mid-July and continue to bloom through most of August, with some plants getting a later start than others. Frequently, when a blooming plant is discovered, you can spot next to it the previous year's stem topped with several seed pods. These orchids reappear fairly reliably year after year.

Note the twist in the ovary. This clearly shows the 180 degree rotation the flower makes from bud to bloom.

This orchid demonstrates quite well the characteristic shared by most of the state's orchids to twist their flowers a full 180 degrees from bud to bloom. If you look closely behind the bloom, you can see the twist in the ovary. Orchids whose flowers do not exhibit this characteristic are called nonresupinate, and the lip is the uppermost petal of the flower. In the case of the club-spur orchid, the flower twists and the lip is in the more usual lower position—its flowers are resupinate. An example of a nonresupinate orchid genus is *Calopogon,* or grass-pink orchids.

I'd be remiss if I did not tell of the first time I saw a club-spur orchid in flower. I was wandering around in one of the state's heritage preserves searching for a rare plant, *Helonias bullata* or swamp pink, whose southernmost extreme is South Carolina. I had spent the day fighting cat briar, rhododendron, and dog hobble and decided that the search would just have to wait for another day. I sat down at the edge of a stream to drink water from my canteen, and beside me were three club-spur orchid plants in full bloom. The sun had poked its way through the heavy canopy of trees and was shining directly on these three plants. It was a sight to see! My camera was in the car, so no photograph was taken, but the picture of that wonderful experience is permanently etched in my mind. It may not be the largest or showiest of the state's orchid species, but it will always be special to me.

A small group of club-spur orchids blooming in the woods near a stream.

NOTES:

Yellow Fringeless Orchid
Golden Frog Arrow

Gymnadeniopsis integra (Nuttall) Lindley

Genus: Gymnadeniopsis—From several Greek words, referring to similarity ("-opsis") to the genus *Gymnadenia*, orchids that have a naked ("gymn") gland ("aden"), meaning the viscidia are free or uncovered.

Species epithet: integra—From Latin word "integer," meaning "entire," referring to the lip which is entire or undivided (unfringed).

Description: This species is quite similar in size and shape to *Platanthera cristata*. The most noticeable difference is that *Gymnadeniopsis integra*'s lip is not fringed around the outer edge as with *P. cristata*, but is finely serrated. Also, the flower color is a pure saffron yellow without any hint of orange shading. The spur is about the same length as the ovary.

This species benefits greatly from prescribed burns. Competition from woody or shrubby species may send it into a nonflowering stage until the next burn opens the area to more sunlight.

In flower: July to early September.

Habitat: Pine savannahs, open bogs, and wet meadows.

Range: Widely scattered along the coastal plain.

Pollinators: Butterflies.

What could be more exciting than walking out into a beautiful longleaf pine savannah and spotting dozens of little yellow "flares" rising above the wire grass? These flares are a brilliant saffron yellow that cannot be mistaken for anything else but *Gymnadeniopsis integra,* also known as yellow fringeless orchid or golden frog arrow.

Typical "Christmas tree" shape of the tiny inflorescence as the flowers begin to open.

Often, they are found blooming beside another similar looking orchid, the crested fringed orchid *(Platanthera cristata)*. Although they are similar, there is one big difference: *P. cristata* has a lip that is heavily fringed while the lip of *Gymnadeniopsis integra* is not fringed but is lightly serrated. In addition, the color of *G. integra* is an intense saffron yellow, which is quite unlike any other flower that would be blooming in the savannah at the same time.

When the inflorescence begins to open, it takes on a conical shape quite like that of a Christmas tree. This conical shape slowly changes to a cylindrical shape as the inflorescence approaches full bloom.

This species is highly dependent on periodic prescribed burns in order to thrive and come back year after year. When the savannah is not burned, these and other plants may become dormant until fire reduces the vegetative competition. Too many years without a burn, and they may not return at all. Fortunately, those in charge of managing the state's forest are now convinced that the use of periodic prescribed burns is a good thing for the forest and all of its residents. In the future, we can hope to see more of these interesting plants.

Sometimes Gymnadeniopsis integra *can be found blooming in small groups of several plants.*

NOTES:

Snowy Orchid

Gymnadeniopsis nivea (Nuttall) Lindley

Genus: Gymnadeniopsis—From several Greek words, referring to similarity ("-opsis") to the genus *Gymnadenia*, orchids that have a naked ("gymn") gland ("aden"), meaning the viscidia are free or uncovered.

Species epithet: nivea—From Latin word "nivea," meaning "snow white," referring to the color of its flowers.

Description: This is a nonresupinate orchid (the lip appears uppermost). The one- to two-foot high plant has a bluish green stem that supports up to fifty one-half-inch, bright white flowers. The narrow lip is usually strongly curved back behind the petals and sepals. The spur extends horizontally behind the flower and curves upward at its tip. The flowers have a decidedly sweet fragrance.

It prefers open, unshaded meadows and roadside ditches and may be found growing in large groups of dozens of plants.

In flower: May to July.

Habitat: Open pine savannahs, wet meadows, bogs, and roadsides.

Range: Generally along the coastal plain.

Pollinators: Butterflies.

I fully expected (hoped) to see a few snowy orchids on an early summer trip to the coastal plain, but to find a ditch full of plants—that was a pleasant surprise. Actually, they were very easy to spot even with other whitish flowers blooming around them. It was the only pure white orchid I had seen. There was no sign of yellow or pink on the petals and sepals. The only other color was the yellow of the pollinia, which are found in the center of each flower.

Showy raceme of the very white and very fragrant snowy orchid (image is slightly larger than life size).

As I bent down to get a close-up photograph, I was unexpectedly greeted by the flower's delicate, floral fragrance. I can only liken it to the aroma of *Epigaea repens* (trailing arbutus)—light and sweet. Most of the state's orchids do not greet us with anything close to such a sweet fragrance—a nice surprise.

The lip is an interesting feature of this orchid. It is the topmost petal; the flower is nonresupinate, meaning that the flower does not twist 180 degrees as it opens. It remains upside down. Of the orchid species found in the South Carolina, only the *Calopogon* species and *Ponthieva racemosa* share this rather unique characteristic. With its intense white color and sweet fragrance, it is a delight to behold and a joy to photograph.

It prefers to grow in damp to wet ditches and meadows. It is not uncommon to find it growing in a few inches of water, especially if it has been a wet spring and summer. If you want to photograph this lovely orchid or just get a closer look, bring your wading boots along and remember: There's no telling what else you might find sharing this habitat.

Large group of Gymnadeniopsis nivea *blooming in a damp roadside ditch.*

NOTES:

Michaux's Orchid

Habenaria quinqueseta (Michaux) Eaton

Genus: Habenaria—From Latin, "habena," meaning "rein" or "strap," referring to the long lip.

Species epithet: quinqueseta—From Latin, meaning "five bristles," referring to the threadlike portions of the petals and lip.

Description: The lip and petals of *Habenaria quinqueseta* are white and are segmented into divisions: the lip has three and the petals each have two. The length of the petal's distal division is usually about two times the length of its proximal division. From a distance, these petal divisions appear to be sections of the lip. This species can easily be confused with *Habenaria macroceratitis*, the long-horned orchid, which does not grow in South Carolina.

The one- to two-foot stem usually has three to fifteen flowers. The flowers are about one and one-half inches long and have spurs that may be five or six inches long.

In flower: Mid-August to early September.

Habitat: Rich, moist hardwoods, pine flatwoods, roadside ditches.

Range: Reported only from the southernmost few coastal counties in the state.

Pollinators: Diurnal moths.

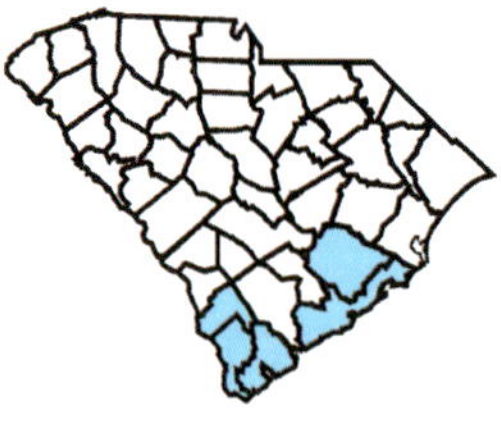

Having just walked into the woods hoping to find examples of the elusive *Habenaria quinqueseta*, commonly known as Michaux's orchid, I was very excited. My excitement changed to disappointment when my companions and I saw a number of plants that were either nonflowering or were fully in seed. In one area, there was a group of ten or twelve plants in a configuration that would have made a knockout picture had I been there two weeks earlier.

In this close-up, it is easy to differentiate the three divisions of the lip and the two divisions of each of the petals.

We continued to search the area and suddenly one in our group exclaimed that he had found a plant with fresh flowers. Not only did it have fresh flowers, but the plant was in perfect form. Photographs of this plant and another smaller plant are included in this chapter.

The plants were about eight to fifteen inches tall and were found sheltered under the branches of a low-growing shrub. Perhaps the protection of this shrub caused these plants to bloom later than the surrounding plants. Whatever the reason, we were in the right place at the right time.

What I find quite interesting about these flowers is that the lip and petals appear, at least to the casual observer, to have a five-division lip with the two petals and dorsal sepal forming the hood over the column. In reality, the lip is divided into just three divisions, and the petals are each divided into two divisions: one division along with the dorsal sepal forms the hood and the other division extends out in a manner similar to the three divisions of the lip.

The flowers of this species closely resemble those of the more southerly *Habenaria macroceratitis,* which is not found in the state. A feature that is used to distinguish between the two is the relative size of the two divisions of the petals. In *H. quinqueseta* the distal portion of the division is nearly twice the length of the proximal portion, whereas in *H. macroceratitis* the distal portion of the division is greater than twice the length of the proximal portion. Sometimes, the length of the spur appears different between the two species, but this characteristic is so variable that is it not a reliable factor.

In any case, *H. quinqueseta* is a good find for the diligent orchid enthusiast. The blooming plants are usually quite robust and will provide the viewer with a beautiful display of white, spiderlike flowers.

When in full bloom, the white flower parts make the plant on the left fairly easy to see in the woods. When in seed, as in the plant on the right, it is more difficult to see since the white petals and lip are withered, and all the remaining flower parts are green or brown.

NOTES:

Water-spider Orchid

Habenaria repens (Nuttall)

Genus: Habenaria—From Latin, "habena," meaning "rein" or "strap," referring to the long lip.

Species epithet: repens—From Latin, meaning "creeping," referring to ability of the plant to put forth new plantlets from the ends of stolons, or runners.

Description: The yellow green leaves of the water-spider orchid are thick and succulent, two to nine inches long, and up to one inch wide. They are narrowly lance-shaped and taper to a narrow point.

The plant's most conspicuous part is the stalk of flowers that occurs at the top. The small flowers are pale green and about three-fourths of an inch across. The petals are narrow, making the flowers resemble small green spiders. It propagates by runners as well as seeds. The plant is erect, growing one to two feet tall.

In flower: April until frost.

Habitat: Marshy shores, lake dams, and sometimes in mats of floating vegetation.

Range: It occurs in about half of the counties, most notably along the coastal plain and into the piedmont.

Pollinators: It may be self-pollinating.

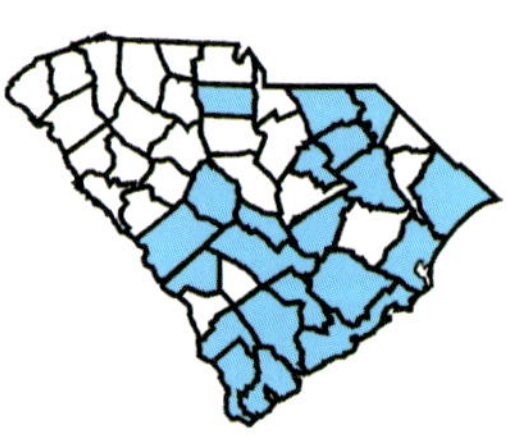

Water-spider is an appropriate name for this orchid's peculiar looking flowers. The petals and narrow, divided lip are stringlike. When viewed head-on, the flower resembles a spider, with the petals and lip appearing as legs splayed against the plant's sepals. As the flower ages, the petals and the section of the column where the petals and lip join turn brown, making its resemblance to a spider more real.

In a year when the season's first frost came late, I have seen this plant blooming in late November. Generally, it begins blooming in April and new plants continue to bloom throughout the summer and fall.

Water-spider orchids in their natural lakeside setting.

The first time I saw this orchid in the wild, I was actually looking for species of the ladies'-tresses orchid *(Spiranthes)*. The water-spider orchids were growing next to the water on a lake dam in Marlboro County. The color of the leaves and flowers was the same color as the other plants it was growing among. The camouflage was perfect.

Water-spider orchids multiply both by spreading seeds and by sending out stolons, or runners. New plants form at the tips of the runners, often creating large clumps of plants. These plants not only grow in the wet spongy soil surrounding ponds and marshes, but often they are found growing in mats of floating vegetation. In any case, water is never far away from this plant.

When backlit, the "spidery" flowers demonstrate how this orchid got its name.

NOTES:

Crested Coralroot Orchid
Cock's-comb Orchid

Hexalectris spicata (Walter) Barnhardt

Genus: Hexalectris—From two Greek words: "hex" refers to the six raised ridges on the lip that resemble a cockscomb, "alectryon."

Species epithet: spicata—From Latin, meaning "spiked," referring to the arrangement of the flowers on the stalk.

Description: The recurved, caramel-colored sepals are streaked with maroon or purple. The petals are the same color but a bit lighter. The lip is streaked with a dark maroon or purple color that merges into a bright orchid pink and is joined at the base by a white to cream-colored column. All this in a one-inch flower. There may be as many as twenty flowers on the one- to two-foot stem.

This species does not produce leaves. It contains no chlorophyll in its stem or flowers and cannot photosynthesize. It is one of the state's several orchid species that receives all of its nourishment from underground fungi (saprophyte).

In flower: July and August.

Habitat: Basic soils in open woods and on ancient shell mounds.

Range: Scattered reports from about half the counties in the state.

Pollinators: Bumblebees.

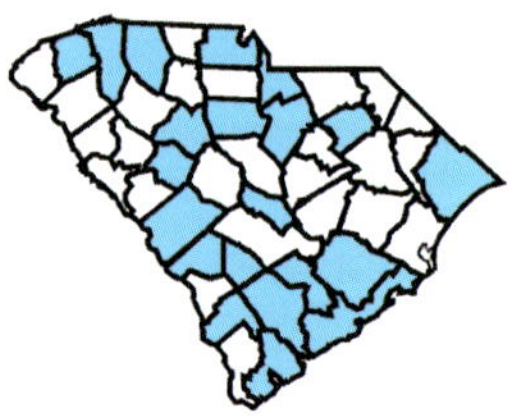

Stately, regal, succulent, downright gorgeous—these are some of the words I've heard describing the flowers of this lovely orchid. Although the colors show up well in the accompanying photographs, these plants are hard to see in the dappled shade of oak-hickory woods. While looking for them popping up through the leaf litter, I have come close to stepping on them.

This orchid prefers basic or calcium-rich soils rather than the acid soils that many of our terrestrial orchids like. In fact, I have never seen it growing under pine trees. At one site, I found more than fifteen plants all blooming at the same time, popping up here and there under immature hickory and oak trees. Several of the plants were as tall as eighteen inches while others were only eight inches tall.

A pair of flowers seen from the side.

Besides requiring a basic soil type, these plants require soil with good drainage. You are most likely to find them on a dry hillside rather than around a boggy streambed.

When you first see these flowers, they will take your breath away. Up close, the color combination is amazing—rich caramel and deep magenta purple with a complement of brownish purple stripes. What a sight. This is one orchid that truly looks like a tropical orchid. Many of our state's native species do not have features that are commonly attributed to nursery-grown orchids.

Hexalectris spicata is also interesting because it is a saprophyte, meaning that it obtains nourishment from decaying organic material. In other words, it contains no chlorophyll and cannot make its own food. With the help of a fungus, it gets its nourishment entirely from rotting vegetation just under the surface of the ground. A few other saprophytic orchid species are found in the state, but I think this is truly the most spectacular.

A trio of Hexalectris spicata *flowers in full bloom.*

NOTES:

Small Whorled Pogonia

Isotria medeoloides (Pursh) Rafinesque

Genus: Isotria—From two Greek words: "isos," meaning "equal," and "treis," meaning "three." It refers to the equal length of the flower's three sepals.

Species epithet: medeoloides—From Greek words "medeola" and "-oides" (similar appearance), referring to the Indian cucumber root, *Medeola virginiana*, which has a similar appearing leaf arrangement.

Description: This species is distinguished by a whorled, umbrella-like arrangement of leaves on a thin, hollow, six- to eight-inch stem. When in flower, the five or six light bluish green leaves point downward. The flower is surrounded by three one-inch sepals that are the same color as the leaves. The three-lobed lip is yellowish green to greenish white and the petals are usually yellowish green. This plant prefers a solitary existence and is not usually found in large clumps or groups. There may be two flowers on a stem.

In flower: May to early June.

Habitat: Mixed deciduous woods and evergreen forests.

Range: This very rare orchid has been reported from only one upstate county.

Pollinators: Self-pollinating.

Federally listed as threatened

My companions and I labored up a steep mountain trail for a couple of hours, then down the other side into the deep woods. We came upon a huge white pine around which were dozens of five and six-leafed plants, some with blossoms or buds, and many more without.

Most of the plants were *Medeola virginiana*, or Indian cucumber root. Those in flower belonged to one of the rarest orchid species in North America, *Isotria medeoloides*, commonly known as the small whorled pogonia. The species name, *medeoloides*, signifies the close resemblance of its leaves and stem to those of the common Indian cucumber root.

Left: A pair of buds that will open in another day or so. Right: Medeola virginiana, *a plant that is often confused with* Isotria medeoloides.

However, there are some fairly obvious differences when both are seen growing side by side. The leaves of the orchid are a frosty blue green whereas the common Indian cucumber root has shiny bright green leaves. The orchid stem is thick and hollow, while the stem of the Indian cucumber root is thin and solid.

The federal government currently lists this orchid as a threatened species. Humans cause the two most threatening dangers to this rare orchid—loss of habitat and specimen collecting.

It is also a species that may seemingly disappear, in what some suspect is a dormant state, only to mysteriously reappear several years later when environmental conditions are just right. Because of its delicate and fragile nature, the continued existence of this species is in doubt.

Isotria medeoloides does not have an especially showy flower, but its rarity and rather unique morphology create an especially wonderful sight if you are lucky enough to come upon them growing in the woods. It will take great diligence and perseverance to keep this orchid in our midst. Let's hope for both.

A two-flowered plant, which is not especially unusual for this species.

NOTES:

Large Whorled Pogonia

Isotria verticillata (Mühlenberg ex Willdenow) Rafinesque

Genus: Isotria—From two Greek words: "isos," meaning "equal," and "treis," meaning "three." It refers to the equal length of the flower's three sepals.

Species epithet: verticillata—From Latin, meaning "whorled," referring to the umbrella-like display of leaves on the stem.

Description: The flower is about four times as wide as it is tall. The width is due to the three long, narrow sepals whose color varies from light green at the base to a very dark purplish brown on the pointed tips. The lip is three-lobed and is usually white on the end and grades to green with purple stripes toward the base. The five leaves that make up the whorl on the foot-long stem are bright green and tend to point upward when the plant is in flower. It is not unusual to find this orchid in small clumps of many plants with only a few in bloom in any one year.

In flower: April to early May.

Habitat: Dry, acid, oak-pine woods.

Range: Reported from three counties in the sandhills and one mountain county.

Pollinators: Small bees.

You could be standing right in front of them and still not see them. *Isotria verticillata* blends in so well with its surroundings, that it just seems to disappear into the background.

This species differs from its closest relative, the small whorled pogonia *(Isotria medeoloides)*, in several ways. The most distinctive difference is the size and color of *I. verticillata*'s large pointed sepals, whose tips are a dark purplish brown color. In addition, *I. verticillata* is almost a foot taller when it blooms.

The long dark sepals and gaping lip cause the flower to resemble a large insect waiting for its prey.

Another difference is that when the plants are in flower, the leaves of *I. verticillata* generally point upward, whereas the leaves of *I. medeoloides* tend to point downward.

The leaves are a shiny bright green, and the hollow stem is a dark purplish brown color. It is for this reason that the plant blends so well into its surroundings.

One population I found was growing on a sloping embankment beside the road. Close by were about a dozen or so pink lady's-slipper orchids *(Cypripedium acaule)*, some in full bloom. Further up the bank were a couple of blooming painted trilliums *(Trillium undulatum)*. What a sight! Sometimes one just gets lucky and is able to see many beautiful wildflower species blooming in the same general area.

Although this species is more plentiful than the small whorled pogonia, it is easily overlooked because it is so well camouflaged. Like many of the other scarce orchid species in the state, loss of habitat is the major danger to its existence.

Whenever orchids are seen blooming on a hillside next to the road, they are growing there because this small strip of land offers the exact requirements they need to survive. Move too far back into the woods, and there is not enough light or moisture for its needs. Widen the road, or spray herbicides for weed control, and the orchid may be lost from that location forever.

Conservation and preservation strategies are required to keep these wonderful plants around for us and our progeny to enjoy. New discoveries in seed germination and propagation may eventually lead to the reintroduction of orchid species that have been extirpated from many areas in the state.

Close-up showing the interior of this lovely flower with the edge of its lip looking like a white bib or apron.

NOTES:

Lily-leaved Twayblade
Mauve Sleekwort

Liparis liliifolia (Linnaeus) L. C. Richard ex Lindley

Genus: Liparis—From Greek, meaning "greasy" or "fat," referring to the greasy or slick appearance of the leaves.

Species epithet: liliifolia—From Latin, meaning "lilia(-um)-leaved," referring to the leaves which resemble those of lily-of-the-valley *(Convallaria)*, previously known as *Lilia*.

Description: The six-inch stem rises from the center of two broad, basal leaves. It supports as many as thirty reddish purple flowers, each composed of a broad, pointed, translucent lip and stringlike dark red petals that hang to the side and below. Two of its three green sepals stretch under the lip and one stretches backward above the lip. The sepals are not flat but are curled lengthwise, giving a rolled appearance.

In flower: Early May to early June.

Habitat: Open, mixed woods and along stream banks.

Range: Reported from a few western, northwestern, and central counties.

Pollinators: Perhaps by flies.

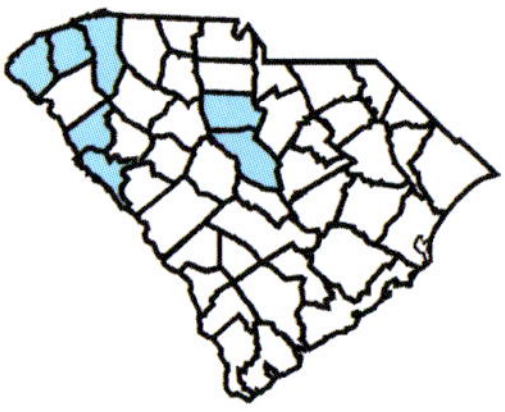

I look forward to walking into the woods on a sunny day in May because I am usually surprised. One day, I was very lucky, and spotted a group of lily-leaved twayblades blooming in the shifting rays of morning sunlight. The tallest of the bloom spikes measured six inches tall and sported about thirty flowers. The two leaves of each plant were bright green and appeared greasy, which is the meaning of the Latin genus name, *Liparis.*

The attractive flowers of this unusual orchid deserve a detailed description. The flowers are attached to the bright green stem by a relatively long, dark red pedicel. They open, as one might expect, from the bottom of the stem to the

The lateral sepals are visible through the translucent lip.

top. Each delicate flower has a rather wide "landing pad" lip that a pollinator can use for support while searching for nectar. The lip is actually a very thin membrane that is so translucent that one can clearly see the lateral sepals below it.

The color of the lip is pale mauve. The stringlike petals that hang under the flower are deep burgundy, while the sepals and column are pale green. This is an attractive combination, but one that makes the flowers well camouflaged in

Showy group of Liparis liliifolia *in dappled sunlight.*

the shade of the woods. To locate this plant, it is best to first look for the bright green leaves; otherwise, it will probably go unnoticed.

Although this particular orchid species has been reported only from the state's piedmont and mountain regions, ideal conditions for it also exist along the inner coastal plain. Diligent searching will probably result in the finding of this orchid species in the coastal counties.

NOTES:

Southern Twayblade

Listera australis Lindley

Genus: Listera—Named for the naturalist Dr. Martin Lister (1638?–1712).

Species epithet: australis—From Latin, meaning "southern," referring to the distribution of this particular species in North America.

Description: This plant is often overlooked because of its size and color. The four- to six-inch stem and one-half-inch flowers are usually reddish purple, pinkish, or purplish green and provide great camouflage in the shaded woods. There may be as many as twenty flowers on a stem, but the usual number is about ten to twelve. Its two green, opposing oval leaves are set about a third of the way up the stem. The flower's two-pronged lip is about one-half inch long, and where the prongs meet, there is a small toothlike projection. The minute petals and sepals are reflexed and rest on either side of the tiny, yellow, buttonlike column.

In flower: February through April.

Habitat: Rich beech and oak-hickory forests and longleaf pine flatwoods.

Range: Counties in the outer coastal plain.

Pollinators: Possibly gnats or other small insects.

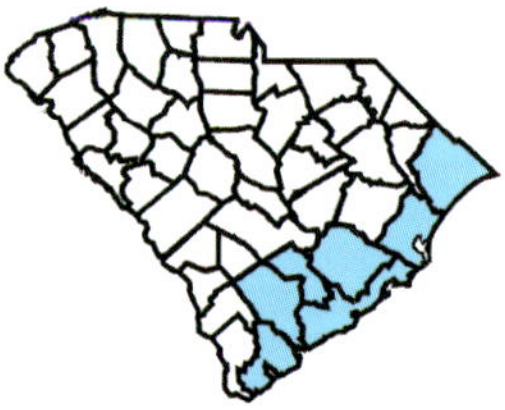

"Boy, they sure are tiny," a photographer friend said. Was she ever right. These tiny little plants blend into their surroundings so well that they are almost impossible to spot when walking through the woods. Because the flowers and stem are the same color as the leaf litter and act as a great camouflage, I have found the best technique for spotting them is to look first for a pair of shiny, dark green leaves.

Listera australis *in bud in early March.*

On one occasion, I was standing in front of a blooming plant and reached around for my camera. When I looked down again, I could not find the plant. It was as if it had disappeared. Only after diligent searching, did I rediscover it.

One of the problems I have with not being able to readily spot these plants is the fear that I might be stepping on plants than I am unable to see. I suppose this is the risk one takes when trying to photograph or observe any of our native plants, but it is still a bit disconcerting.

Close-up showing flower's two-lobed lip.

Upon close inspection, the flower exhibits a very distinctive lip. It is relatively long in comparison to the extremely tiny petals and sepals. It is divided into two pointed lobes that extend about one-half to two-thirds the length of the lip. Where the lobes join, there is a tiny protuberance or tooth, which is present on almost all of the species in the genus *Listera*.

The flowers can be either purplish green, pinkish purple, dark maroon, greenish tan, or any color in between. In addition, different plants growing in the same area may exhibit any of these colors.

Since this is one of the first orchids to bloom in the calendar year, you will have to start looking early. During a mild winter in South Carolina, they have been known to bloom as early as February. If you are persistent and find this orchid in the wild, you will surely enjoy the delicate flowers as well as this orchid's ability to hide from inquisitive eyes.

NOTES:

Small's Twayblade
Kidney-leaved Twayblade

Listera smallii Wiegand

Genus: Listera—Named for the naturalist Dr. Martin Lister (1638?–1712).

Species epithet: smallii—Named for J. K. Small, who, along with his associate A. A. Heller, discovered the plant in 1891 in western North Carolina.

Description: The flowers are made inconspicuous due to their small size and subdued earth colors. On either side of the base of the lip is a small glandlike structure. The lip broadens into two rounded, flat lobes toward the tip and has a tiny tooth in the middle of the notch between the lobes. The thin, pubescent stem may reach as high as eight inches. The leaves are in the shape of a kidney, giving rise to another common name, kidney-leaved twayblade.

In flower: June through July.

Habitat: Near streams, growing under rhododendron and mountain laurel.

Range: Rare. It is reported from the upper reaches of only two of South Carolina's mountain counties.

Pollinators: Unknown.

Talk about a tough little orchid to locate—this is one of the rarest in the state. It is not only hard to find this orchid, but once you do find a suitable habitat, the plant's coloration makes it almost impossible to spot. Its greenish brown lip and petals blend in perfectly with the leaf litter under a rhododendron's branches. In fact, the easiest way to spot this plant is to look for the single pair of bright green leaves.

It is called a twayblade for an obvious reason: It has two leaves per plant. The leaves are kidney-shaped, which gives rise to the name kidney-leaved twayblade. The stem protrudes between the two shiny green leaves at the point where they join. The entire plant is only a few inches tall and seems to be very spindly and fragile. If it received more sunlight, it might be more vigorous, but that is not its preference.

Except for the pair of green leaves, this tiny orchid is impossible to spot in deep shade.

The flower's tiny greenish brown petals are narrow and radiate outward from the center. The lip is flattened and is narrowest where it joins the other petals. The lip is composed of two lobes, between which is a tiny toothlike protuberance.

The plants in the photographs in this chapter were found while I was searching for the headwaters of Matthew's Creek in the Watson-Cooper Heritage Preserve in upper Greenville County. After hacking my way through an incredibly dense thicket of mountain laurel *(Kalmia latifolia)* and rhododendron *(Rhododendron maximum)* near the creek, I sat down to take a break and drink

Six Small's twayblade orchid plants—only three of which are in flower.

some water. When I looked down, there were about a dozen Small's twayblade orchid plants—a few in full bloom. If I had been searching for these plants, I never would have found them. And if I had to go back to that exact spot, I doubt that I could retrace my steps. Just another very lucky day. I'm glad I remembered to pack my camera.

NOTES:

Florida Adder's-mouth Orchid

Malaxis spicata Swartz

Genus: Malaxis—From Greek, meaning "soft," referring to the texture of the leaves.

Species epithet: spicata—From Latin, meaning "spicate," referring to the arrangement of the flowers on the stalk.

Description: All parts of the plant are green except the lips of the tiny flowers, which are usually some shade of orange or brown. The flowers are arranged in a spike and usually open from the bottom to the top of the raceme as the stem grows upward. The stem may reach from four to ten inches in length and is clasped toward its base by two nearly opposite oval-shaped leaves. The topmost leaf is about one-half inch above the lowermost leaf.

In flower: July to September.

Habitat: Rich, damp woods, swamps, and the floodplains of creeks.

Range: Found in scattered locations along the coastal plain.

Pollinators: It is believed to be pollinated by small flies or gnats.

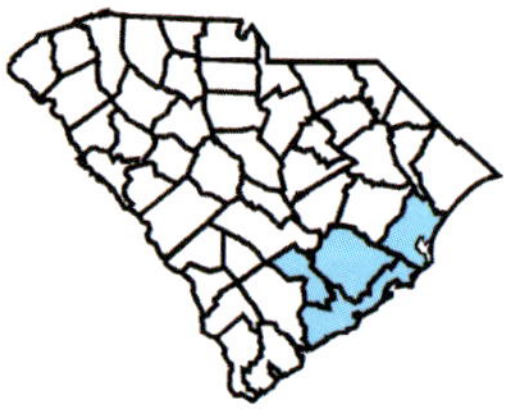

If you are looking for *Malaxis spicata*, bring your boots. These plants love to have their feet wet, and you are likely to get yours wet looking for them. This species has even been seen growing on large floating logs and decaying stumps deep within the swamp.

Tall raceme with dozens of tiny orange and green flowers.

This orchid is different from its cousin, *Malaxis unifolia*, in several respects. First, *M. spicata* usually is found with two shiny clasping leaves at the base of the stem; *M. unifolia* has a single clasping leaf. Second, *M. spicata* has a spiked or cone-shaped raceme, whereas *M. unifolia* has a cylindrical raceme whose length increases dramatically as the flowers begin to open. Third, the flowers of *M. spicata* are some shade of orange or brown, whereas the flowers of *M. unifolia* are always green or yellow green.

Both species exhibit a stem that swells just under the surface of the soil (a pseudobulb), and both species have flowers that continue opening over a period of a couple of months. In the photograph to the left, you can see that the lowermost flower has been fertilized and has begun to produce seeds even while the uppermost flower buds have not yet opened.

Malaxis spicata flowers require magnification to be fully appreciated. The disclike lip is orange or brown and usually points outward or downward under the greenish

Notice the small pseudobulb at bottom of this eighteen-inch-tall plant.

sepals. There may be as few as a dozen flowers on a single eight-inch stem. Much larger plants exist, as well. In their book *Wild Orchids of Florida*, Brown and Folsom reported seeing a single plant that was twenty-one inches tall with more than a hundred flowers.

NOTES:

Green Adder's-mouth Orchid

Malaxis unifolia Michaux

Genus: Malaxis—From Greek, meaning "soft," referring to the texture of the leaves.

Species epithet: unifolia—From Latin prefix "uni" and the word "folia," meaning "one leaf," referring to the single leaf of each plant.

Description: This species has the smallest flowers of any South Carolina orchid. The flower is less than one-eighth inch wide and has a toothed lip. All parts of the plant, including the flowers, are green. The flowers are arranged in a spiral and open from the outer edge of the spiral as the stem grows upward. The stem may reach from four to ten inches in length and is clasped toward its base by a single oval-shaped leaf.

In flower: Mid to late May through July.

Habitat: Moist to dry mixed woods and thickets.

Range: Found in scattered locations from the mountains to the coastal plain.

Pollinators: It is believed to be pollinated by small flies or gnats.

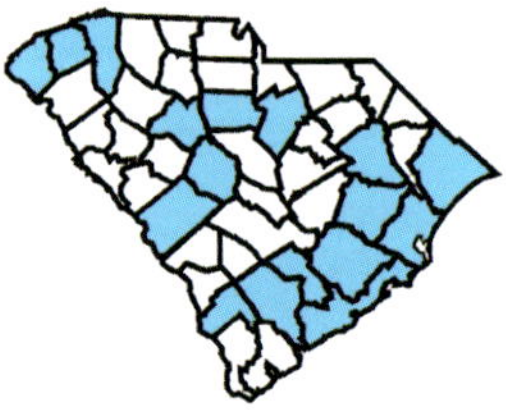

Although this species is considered to be rather scarce in the state, this is probably due to the difficulty of spotting it in the edges of meadows and under the low-growing foliage in mixed woods. Its overall range stretches from Canada's maritime provinces to central Florida, yet its specific distributions are very thinly scattered within this range.

Malaxis unifolia *in bud in early May. This plant is still weeks away from being in full bloom.*

As with many of the orchids that I have photographed, I came across this species accidentally. I was photographing pink lady's-slipper orchids *(Cypripedium acaule)* in an upstate heritage preserve. That particular year, *Malaxis unifolia* already had bloomed and had begun to produce seed capsules, so I marked the location. The next year, I came back to the same spot early enough to see it in bud.

Subsequent weekly trips provided me the opportunity to watch it mature and finally to photograph it at its peak. It was a relatively slow bloomer, and I was able to enjoy it for several weeks as the stem lengthened and the flowers opened sequentially.

It is a diminutive species. The flowers are very tiny, and in order to appreciate them to the fullest in the field, a magnifying glass is required. The plants pictured on the previous page are only about four to five inches tall—not a very big plant for an orchid.

The group that I visit yearly consists of about twenty plants. They grow in an area of about three feet square and are located under the branches of an immature, low-growing oak tree. You can see why this group might be easy to miss. I have been unable to locate any other plants in the same general area, although I haven't given up the search.

It is the diversity of the state's orchid species that intrigues me the most, and *M. unifolia* is quite interesting. It is well worth your while to find a location where it is growing. Be sure to bring a magnifying glass so that you can appreciate the beauty of its tiny flowers up close.

Close-up of a green adder's-mouth orchid plant in dappled sunlight.

NOTES:

Platanthera

The genus *Platanthera* is represented in South Carolina by eight species. It is the largest genus of orchids found in the United States and Canada. The name is derived from two Greek words: "platys" meaning "broad" and "anthera" meaning "anther," which refers to the pollen-producing part of a flower.

L. C. Richard originally proposed the genus *Platanthera* in 1818, but numerous authors reduced it to synonymy within *Habenaria* until Luer (1972, 1975) resurrected the genus and made several new combinations. After this reinstatement, *Habenaria* was restricted primarily to tropical species. The characteristic distinguishing the two genera is the placement of the pollinia within the flower, but in South Carolina, the presence of tubers or tuberoid roots on species of *Habenaria* and elongated roots on *Platanthera* helps to separate them.

Since about 15 percent of the state's orchid species and hybrids fall within the genus *Platanthera*, it is instructive to describe some of the common characteristics.

First, the flower of each species has a tubelike elongation (spur) at the base of the lip that contains nectar, which attracts insects. Equipped with a long, probing proboscus or tongue, an insect drinks the sweet nectar. In so doing, it picks up the pollinia, which is then transported to the next flower it visits.

Second, many, but not all, of the included species are considered "fringed orchids" due to the heavy fringing along the edges of the lip and petals. Some species are more heavily fringed than others, namely *Platanthera lacera, P. psycodes,* and *P. ciliaris* (see images to the right). This effect is often compounded by an additional splitting or lobing of the lip wherein it is further divided into separate sections.

The third characteristic common to this genus is the similar appearance of the leaves. A majority of the *Platanthera* species found in South Carolina have lanceolate (lance-shaped) leaves. The leaves are much larger at the base of the plant and become smaller or are almost nonexistent or bractlike toward the tip of the stem.

The last characteristic that is most common is the way the flowers appear on the stem. Each of the species in the genus *Platanthera* has its flowers arranged in a raceme or grouping of separate stalked flowers on the top third of the stem. There may be as few as six to ten flowers or as many as 100 or more per stem, depending on the species and on the environmental conditions of the current or previous growing season. A species such as *P. integrilabia* generally does not have more than a dozen flowers, whereas *P. psycodes* may commonly have more than 100 flowers per stem.

This genus contains some of South Carolina's loveliest orchids. The variety of form as well as color in *Platanthera* lends excitement and anticipation to every field trip where they are sought.

Platanthera lacera

Platanthera psycodes

Platanthera ciliaris

NOTES:

White Fringed Orchid

Platanthera blephariglottis (Willdenow) Lindley

Genus: Platanthera—From Greek "platys," meaning "broad," and "anthera," meaning "anther," referring to the pollen-producing part of a flower.

Species epithet: blephariglottis—From Greek words "blepharis," meaning "eyelash" and "glottis," meaning "mouth." Together they refer to the fringed nature of the lip.

Description: The stem, which supports a raceme of between thirty and sixty flowers, is from fifteen to thirty inches tall. It bears a few narrow pointed leaves from the base to about one-third the length of the stem. From that point to the raceme, the leaves become tiny and almost like bracts.

The bright white flowers are about one-half inch across and are composed of two reflexed lateral sepals, a dorsal sepal that acts as a "hood," and two narrow, fringe-tipped petals. The half-inch-long narrow lip is bordered by a fine, feathery fringe. Each flower has a spur that is about three times as long as the lip. This spur descends from the base of the lip and forms the nectary.

In flower: July to September.

Habitat: Wet ditches, pine savannahs, and bogs.

Range: Mostly along the coastal plain *(P. blephariglottis* var. *conspicua)*, but also in the sandhills *(P. blephariglottis* var. *blephariglottis)*.

Pollinators: Butterflies and moths.

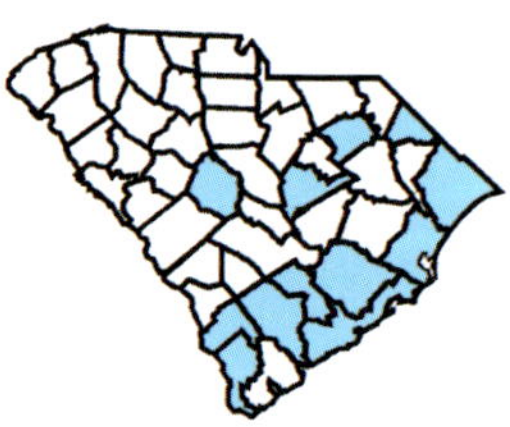

The bright white flowers are an unmistakable characteristic of the white fringed orchid, which makes it stand out in its surroundings. Against the dark green of grasses and other plants, it waves in the wind like a ball of popcorn on a stick. Frequently, it is taller than the surrounding foliage, which makes it even more visible from a distance.

Although this orchid can be found in the higher elevations in neighboring states, you more likely will discover it while visiting the savannahs and backwoods of the coastal plain.

There are differences between white fringed orchids that grow inland or in the northern states and those found along the coastal plain of the Carolinas. The inland and northern variety, *P. blephariglottis* var. *blephariglottis*, the northern white fringed orchid, has a shorter fringe and shorter spur, whereas the

Note the long spurs and fringe on this group of white fringed orchid flowers.

southeastern coastal variety, *P. blephariglottis* var. *conspicua* (meaning "conspicuous"), the southern white fringed orchid, has a finer, more filiform fringe and a distinct isthmus at the base of the lip. The spur is also considerably longer—often about three inches. There are several other differences, but these are the most obvious. They are also pollinated by two different species of butterflies.

Unusually large grouping of white fringed orchid flowers just beginning to bloom.

White fringed orchid flower from a plant that exhibits flowers with a relatively short, thin fringe.

NOTES:

The white fringed orchid closely resembles its cousin, the yellow fringed orchid *(P. ciliaris)*. The flower size and petal and sepal morphology are the same, but the fringe length is different. In some plants, the fringe of the white fringed orchid may be significantly shorter.

In my experience, the white fringed orchid likes its feet a little wetter than its close relatives. Also, I have not seen the large drifts of plants that are frequently found with the yellow fringed orchid. However, none of these distinctions detracts from the beauty of this lovely plant. More than once while driving, I have succumbed to the urge to slam on my brakes after spotting one of these white beauties waving in the wind.

It is also quite interesting to see this orchid blooming beside the yellow fringed orchid *(P. ciliaris)* and the crested yellow fringed orchid *(P. cristata)*. Quite a show, indeed, white, orange, and bright yellow orange.

Yellow Fringed Orchid

Platanthera ciliaris (Linnaeus) Lindley

Genus: Platanthera—From Greek "platys," meaning "broad," and "anthera," meaning "anther," referring to the pollen-producing part of a flower.

Species epithet: ciliaris—From Latin "ciliaris," meaning "fringed."

Description: The stem, which supports a raceme of between thirty and sixty flowers, is from twelve to thirty inches tall. It bears a few narrow pointed leaves from the base to about one-third the length of the stem. From that point to the raceme, the leaves become tiny and almost like bracts.

The yellow to orange flowers are about one-half inch across and are composed of two reflexed lateral sepals, a dorsal sepal that acts as a "hood," and two narrow, fringe-tipped petals that protrude from under the hood. The half-inch-long narrow lip is completely bordered by a fine feathery fringing. Each flower has a spur that is about two to three times as long as the lip. This spur descends from the base of the lip and forms the nectary.

In flower: July to September.

Habitat: Bogs, meadows, damp roadside ditches, and open sandy woods.

Range: Scattered in about half the counties from the mountains to the coastal plain.

Pollinators: Large butterflies and moths.

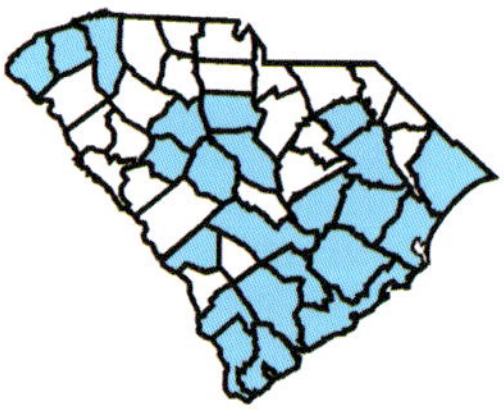

Little orange rockets—that's what yellow fringed orchids look like. If you are traveling fast down the highway, you probably won't see these beautiful plants unless they occur in a large group. One continuing danger for this species, aside from greedy and thoughtless orchid hunters, is being mowed down by road crews. They have a knack for sprouting up just off the highway or just off the cart path on golf courses. Fortunately for those of us who appreciate these beautiful plants, many are found growing safely in meadows, open pine woods, and in power line clearings.

In a month's time, I watched a particular group form buds and finally bloom. If patience is not your virtue, don't try this; it can become very frustrating.

Flowers as seen directly from above.

Once the flowers begin to open, the plant puts on a spectacular show. The tiny yellow orange (I would describe the color as cantaloupe) flowers open in succession from the bottom of the bud stalk to the top; all flowers stay fresh looking until the last bud is open. When the plant is in full bloom, it almost mimics an orange feather duster. The stem is from twelve to thirty inches tall and sports a cluster of thirty to sixty flowers.

The flower's lateral sepals are reflexed or bent slightly backward. The two upper petals are tiny, but if you look closely, you will see a jagged fringe on the tip of each petal. The dorsal sepal forms a hood over the column, seeming to protect it from some unknown danger. The most spectacular part of the flower is the lip. It is so heavily fringed that it appears feathery. Just like snowflakes, no two lips have the same fringing pattern, even among flowers blooming on the same stem. Stretching back from the base of the lip is a relatively long spur where the nectar is stored. This spur may be three times the length of the slender lip. Spur length is used to differentiate between the several *Platanthera* species that exhibit similar color and shape.

To some wildflower enthusiasts, this is the most beautiful of South Carolina's orchid species. Certainly, I cannot imagine a more delicate and colorful wildflower that can be seen growing along the roadside. When you get a chance, use a magnifier to examine the flower closely. You may find that it is your favorite orchid species as well.

Group of Platanthera ciliaris *blooming in the sun along the side of the road.*

NOTES:

Crested Fringed Orchid

Platanthera cristata (Michaux) Lindley

Genus: Platanthera—From Greek "platys," meaning "broad," and "anthera," meaning "anther," referring to the pollen-producing part of a flower.

Species epithet: cristata—From Latin, "cristatus" meaning "crested," referring to the crests on the petals.

Description: The eight- to twelve-inch stem supports a cluster of up to eighty tiny golden yellow or saffron-colored flowers. These flowers are about one-third-inch across and are tightly clustered on the stem. The lip is concave and is in front of a spur whose length is less than the length of the supporting ovary or pedicel. The short spur is a determining characteristic when comparing it with its close look-alike, *Platanthera ciliaris*, the yellow fringed orchid.

Along the coastal plain, it is more common than *P. ciliaris,* where they are sometimes found inhabiting the same locations.

In flower: July through September.

Habitat: Bogs, swamps, wet meadows and pine savannahs.

Range: Found in about one-third of the state's counties, mostly along the coastal plain.

Pollinators: Bumblebees.

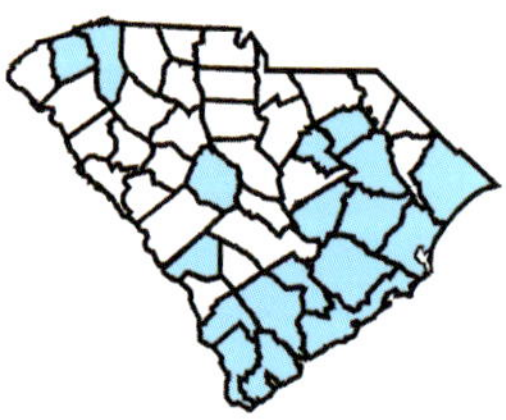

Unless you are looking in a pine savannah about a year after a recent burn, you will have a difficult time spotting this smallish orchid. Often, it is shorter than the surrounding foliage that grows after a burn.

Its color is quite unmistakable—a golden yellow, quite different from its cousin, the yellow fringed orchid *(Platanthera ciliaris)*. Although *P. cristata* shares many of the characteristics with its larger cousin, it is quite identifiable on its own merits.

Two stems blooming on a ditch bank.

The length of the spur is the most readily identifiable characteristic. In *P. cristata*, the spur is shorter than the ovary portion that connects the flower to the stem. In *P. ciliaris*, the spur is much longer that the ovary, sometimes as much as twice as long or longer. The flowers are about half the size of *P. ciliaris* and do not exhibit the extensive fringing of this closely related species.

To me, the flowers of *P. cristata* do not appear to fully open. By this, I mean the unfolding of the fringed lip. It always seems to be just short of lying flat and straight as in *P. ciliaris*. Also, the fringe appears to be curled or twisted, even after the flowers have been open for a week or more.

In no way does this detract from the beauty of this orchid, for it is truly a little light in the dark recesses of the brush or grass that usually surrounds it.

On a recent trip to one of the longleaf pine savannahs in the lowcountry, I stopped to take a photograph of an especially beautiful savannah which had received annual burns in the last couple of years. It showed a beautiful and uniform stand of grasses. I stepped off the road and into the ditch to take a picture, and suddenly out of the corner of my eye I spotted a bright yellow orange plume in the grass. It was a crested fringed orchid. Upon careful searching, I was able to find about ten more plants in flower; none of which could be seen from the road. I was lucky that I chose that very spot to take photographs.

This experience is not unusual for me. It is this type of luck that often brings the most surprises. It doesn't hurt to be in the right place, though. Careful diligence and a bit of luck can bring you all of the flowers that you are searching for.

Close-up of Platanthera cristata. *Note the concave lip and rounded hood.*

NOTES:

Tubercled Orchid
Southern Rein Orchid

Platanthera flava (Linnaeus) Lindley var. *flava*

Genus: Platanthera—From Greek "platys," meaning "broad," and "anthera," meaning "anther," referring to the pollen-producing part of a flower.

Species epithet: flava—From Latin, meaning "yellow," referring to the color of the flowers.

Description: This stiff, yellow green flowered species has a distinctive tubercle, or "bump," at the center of the base of the lip of each quarter-inch, spurred flower. Plants growing in bright sun have yellow green leaves, and the flowers are compact or crowded along the stem. Plants growing in shade have darker green leaves and more space between the flowers.

There is a more northern variety *(Platanthera flava* var. *herbiola)* that is distinguished by its lighter colored flowers and significantly longer flower bracts; however, it has not been confirmed from South Carolina.

In flower: March to September.

Habitat: Along the floodplain of creeks and in bogs, marshes, and wet meadows.

Range: Mostly along the coastal plain and inner coastal plain.

Pollinators: Moths and mosquitoes.

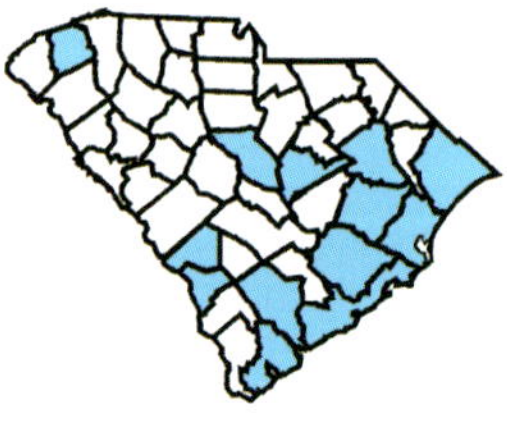

If you like stomping around in the muck and mud of the swamp, and if you like fighting mosquitoes, deer flies, and snakes, then you will love hunting for *Platanthera flava* var. *flava*. While capturing the images in this chapter, I spotted a copperhead snake *(Agkistrodon contortrix)* coiled up under a swamp tupelo *(Nyssa sylvatica)*. Orchid photography is not for the faint of heart.

Platanthera flava var. *herbiola* is the more northerly variety of this species. It is commonly found from the mountains of North Carolina to the provinces of eastern Canada. The primary differences between the two varieties are that the flowers on *P. flava* var. *herbiola* have a slightly different lip shape and the flower bracts are much longer than the flower.

Swollen ovaries of Platanthera flava *indicating seed production.*

Platanthera flava var. *flava* is also commonly known as the tubercled orchid. It acquired this name because of the bump or tubercle that is seen in the upper center of the lip of each flower. Since the flowers are small, magnification is required to appreciate this feature. In other respects, the flowers are rather nondescript. The color of the petals, sepals, stem, and leaves is yellow green.

The color of the lip varies from yellow to yellow green. I suspect that this variation is due, in part, to the amount of sun the plant receives during the day. The more shaded plants have green lips, while the ones in sunnier locations tend to be more yellow.

The bloom time for this species is quite long compared to some other orchids. The plants begin

Notice the bump, or tubercle, on the lip of each flower. It is this tubercle that prompted one of the common names.

flowering in June or July. By August, they have begun to produce seeds; however, the flower is persistent. This is fortunate for those of us who cannot always be there at the right place and time to view these wonders of nature at their full peak.

NOTES:

White Fringeless Orchid
Monkey-face Orchid

Platanthera integrilabia (Correll) Luer

Genus: Platanthera—From Greek "platys," meaning "broad," and "anthera," meaning "anther," referring to the pollen-producing part of a flower.

Species epithet: integrilabia—From two Latin words "integer," meaning "undivided" or "entire," and "labia," meaning "lip," referring to the flower's unfringed or undivided lip.

Description: This species is superficially similar to *Platanthera blephariglottis* var. *conspicua,* except that the lip of *P. integrilabia* is entire or unfringed. The flowers are large and white. The plants are small, and it is not uncommon for only a few plants in a large group to bloom in any one year.

The raceme is loosely flowered compared to its cousin *P. blephariglottis* and usually has less than a dozen blooms. The exceedingly long spur may be up to three inches long. This species usually prefers deep shade within the forest.

In flower: Early August.

Habitat: Shaded mountain bogs and wet woods.

Range: Very rare. Reported only from Greenville County.

Pollinators: Specialized moths.

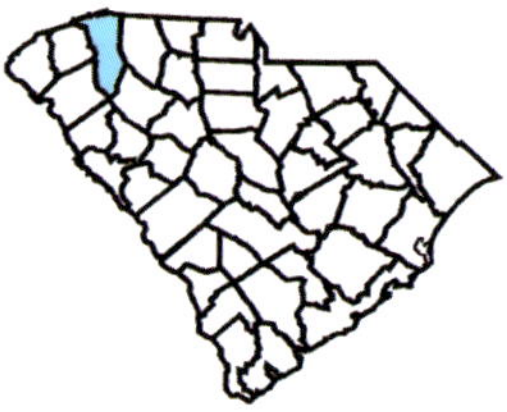

Platanthera integrilabia is one of the truly rare orchids which grows in South Carolina and in a few other states as well. It gets its name from the unfringed or undivided nature of its flower's lip. It is quite similar in appearance to the southern white fringed orchid *(P. blephariglottis* var. *conspicua)*, which is also found in the state.

Notice the three-inch spur and fringeless lip on each flower.

A subtle difference is the length of *P. integrilabia*'s spur. It can be as long as three inches. Nectar is found at the bottom of the spur, but only a moth or butterfly that has a very long proboscis can collect it. I have seen common swallowtail butterflies visit this plant, but I doubt that they are capable of getting much of a reward for their efforts.

Also like its cousin the southern white fringed orchid *(P. blephariglottis* var. *conspicua)*, the white fringeless orchid likes a very wet environment. The plants pictured in this chapter were found in a deeply shaded mountain bog. I noticed that the largest blooms, however, were found on plants at the edge of the bog, where they receive a bit more sunlight than the other plants in the shaded, central portion of the bog.

Another orchid that is often found growing in the same environment as *P. integrilabia* is the hardy club-spur orchid *(Gymnadeniopsis clavellata)*. Although these two species grow together and bloom at the same time, no hybrids have been reported. There may be a genetic barrier that prevents hybridization.

You may find many white fringeless orchid plants inhabiting a relatively small area, but in any one year, I have noticed only a small percentage in bloom. Knowing this, it was especially gratifying to see a number of plants blooming together (pictured below). The nonblooming plants usually show only a single straplike leaf above ground.

Small group of Platanthera integrilabia *blooming along an old fence line deep in a shaded mountain bog.*

NOTES:

Ragged Fringed Orchid
Green Fringed Orchid

Platanthera lacera (Michaux) G. Don ex Sweet

Genus: Platanthera—From Greek "platys," meaning "broad," and "anthera," meaning "anther," referring to the pollen-producing part of a flower.

Species epithet: lacera—From Latin "lacer," meaning "torn," referring to the deep, ragged fringing of the flower's lip.

Description: The half-inch-wide pale yellow to greenish yellow flowers of this species are very heavily fringed. The lip is divided into three lobes each consisting of hairlike separations. A one-inch spur curves downward behind the lip. The loosely spaced flowers are similar to *Habenaria repens* except that the three lobes of the lip in *H. repens* are not further divided.

The plant is from ten inches to two feet tall and usually has from four to six narrow, pointed leaves.

In flower: June to August.

Habitat: Roadside ditches, wet meadows, marshes, and bogs.

Range: In scattered locations across the state.

Pollinators: Moths.

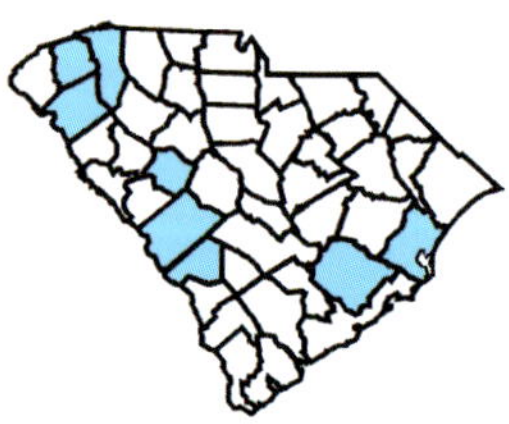

If you want to find *Platanthera lacera*, be prepared to get your feet wet. In South Carolina, they love moist, boggy habitats, places where you may find yourself ankle-deep in sphagnum. These plants are not tall, generally one to two feet high, but they are usually easy to find among the surrounding vegetation due to the light color of the flower's lip.

Flowers on the raceme are loosely spaced.

Their preferred environment is also suitable for other orchid species. It is not unusual to find scattered groups of common grass-pink *(Calopogon tuberosus)* and rose pogonia *(Pogonia ophioglossoides)* close by.

Unlike some of the other fringed orchids of the South or southeast, *Platanthera lacera* tends not to form large compact groups, but rather is found as scattered single plants. From my perspective, this just makes spotting this plant in the tall grasses of a damp meadow or bog even more special.

You really cannot appreciate the beauty of the flower unless you inspect it through a magnifier. The delicate, threadlike fringe of the lip is what gives it the common name, ragged fringed orchid. The tiny tendrils twist and turn in odd directions as they separate from the three main lobes of the lip.

In contrast to the small purple fringed orchid *(P. psycodes)* or the yellow fringed orchid *(P. ciliaris)*, the flowers are not closely packed on the raceme but appear loosely spaced for its entire length—not an unpleasant presentation.

This orchid is not routinely sought after by wildflower enthusiasts because it is does not present strikingly beautiful or colorful flowers, but that shouldn't stop an orchid lover from going to extremes to find it. Be persistent in your search, and you will be rewarded.

Close-up showing the ragged lip of Platanthera lacera.

NOTES:

Purple Fringeless Orchid

Platanthera peramoena (Asa Gray) Asa Gray

Genus: Platanthera—From Greek "platys," meaning "broad," and "anthera," meaning "anther," referring to the pollen-producing part of a flower.

Species epithet: peramoena—From Latin "peramoena," loosely meaning "most delightful."

Description: The three-quarter-inch flowers of this species are superficially similar in size and color to the small purple fringed orchid *(P. psycodes),* except the lip of *P. peramoena* exhibits no fringing. The lip is divided into three lobes, the outer edges of which have small teethlike separations. The middle lobe is larger and has a cleft or notch in the center. The color of the flower is a bright "bubble gum" pink. It is quite easily mistaken for the tall phlox *(Phlox paniculata),* among which it is sometimes found growing.

The flower stem is about two feet tall (rarely three) and is clasped at its lower section by vertical leaves that decrease in size from the bottom to the top of the stem.

In flower: July to August.

Habitat: Wet fields, meadows, and ditches.

Range: Rare. Reported only from Greenville County.

Pollinators: Certain moths and butterflies.

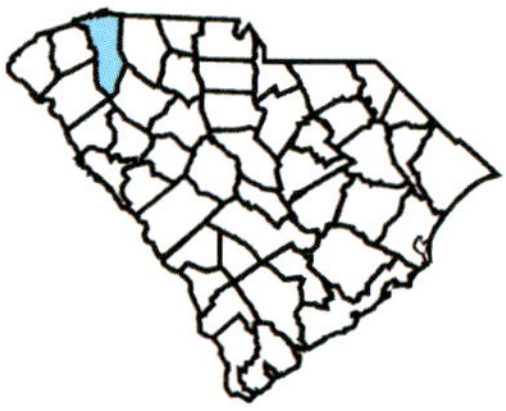

A tall raceme crammed with dozens of beautiful deep rose-pink flowers.

Even while riding along the highway at fifty-five miles per hour, you can easily spot this lovely orchid blooming in ditches and meadow edges. The color is usually some shade of intense rose pink, often described as bubble gum pink.

The flowers are loosely to tightly packed along the length of the cylindrical raceme, which may be eight to twelve inches in length and rise to three feet above the ground. It is very showy and imposing. The display is similar to that of the small purple fringed orchid *(Platanthera psycodes)*, but more striking.

Besides the color, the main difference between *P. peramoena* and *P. psycodes* is that *P. peramoena* totally lacks fringing on its flower parts. Instead of fringing, it has very tiny toothlike serrations along the edges of its lip and petals. However, it brings the ditches and meadows alive with color.

Unfortunately, living in ditches and along the edges of meadows can be dangerous, especially for an orchid. While capturing the images pictured in this chapter, a photographer friend and I found ourselves just ahead of mowing equipment that was being used to clear the area. Afterwards, dozens of beautiful orchids lay in the ditch alongside the grasses and small willows that began the day upright.

Since this species is not protected by legislation, it is at the mercy of the landowners whether it thrives and is around to see another year. Because this species likes to grow out in the open where it is vulnerable to mowing and to collecting by unscrupulous orchid collectors, its future is not as rosy as its lovely flowers.

The flowers on this particular plant are wide and full and larger than the typical Platanthera peramoena *flowers.*

NOTES:

Small Purple Fringed Orchid
Butterfly Orchid

Platanthera psycodes (Linnaeus) Lindley

Genus: Platanthera—From Greek "platys," meaning "broad," and "anthera," meaning "anther," referring to the pollen-producing part of a flower.

Species epithet: psycodes—From Greek "psyche," meaning "butterfly" or "moth," referring to the appearance of its petals.

Description: This species may reach as high as two or three feet, but it is usually about fifteen to eighteen inches tall. The flower raceme may contain as few as a dozen or as many as 100 or more half-inch flowers. The lip of the flower is divided into three lobes, each heavily fringed. The petals are lightly fringed and may be raised upright. The lateral sepals may be slightly or acutely reflexed or bent backward. The opening to the nectary is usually barbell-shaped.

Color variation in this species is remarkable. It is not uncommon to find large groups where each plant is a different color, deep pink to rose magenta to purple. Some bicolor flowers have been observed, where the lip is white and all other flower parts are pink or purple (forma *bicolor*). Pure white flowers are rare.

In flower: Late June to mid-July.

Habitat: Wet meadows and roadside ditches near spruce forests.

Range: Rare. Reported only from Oconee County.

Pollinators: Butterflies and moths.

Of the two purple fringed *Platanthera* species, *P. psycodes* was originally described in 1753, and *P. grandiflora* (not found in South Carolina) was described in 1824. In the ensuing years, confusion between these two similar species led to much taxonomic lumping. In 1974, Warren Stoutamire published a definitive paper supporting the separation of the two species.

According to Stanley Bentley in *Native Orchids of the Southern Appalachian Mountains*, the main differentiating characteristic used in field comparisons is the shape of the nectary opening. The large purple fringed orchid has a large and completely round opening, while the opening of the small purple fringed orchid is smaller and dumbbell-shaped.

Lovely group of small purple fringed orchids on a hillside.

There are other characteristics that seem to occur more in one species than the other, such as larger plant or flower size *(P. grandiflora)* and acutely reflexed sepals *(P. psycodes).* But the significant overlap of these characteristics between the species makes them unreliable.

Seeing a large population of these lovely orchids is breathtaking. As you approach the stems waving in the wind, it is as if someone attempted to capture every imaginable shade of pink and purple and still was not satisfied. Now and then, you can see flowers with multiple shades where the lip is lighter than the petals and sepals.

Plant size is also quite variable. Plants growing where there is more sunlight may be two or more feet tall with nearly 100 flowers, while plants growing under trees often are only six to eight inches tall with only a dozen flowers.

When you look at the flower up close, its complexity is apparent. The heavy fringing of the three-lobed lip makes each flower slightly different from another, even when on the same stem. The petals and the dorsal sepal meet to form a hood over the opening to the nectary. Viewing the flower from the side, you notice the spur, which juts out and downward from the back of the flower.

All things considered, the small purple fringed orchid is one of the showiest in the state.

Close-up of small purple fringed orchid flowers.

NOTES:

Rose Pogonia
Snake Mouth Orchid

Pogonia ophioglossoides (Linnaeus) Ker-Gawler

Genus: *Pogonia*—from Greek, meaning "bearded," referring to the heavily fringed or bearded lip.

Species epithet: *ophioglossoides*—from three Greek words: "ophis," meaning "snake," "glossa," meaning "tongue," and "eidos," meaning "resembling." But it especially refers to the plant's resemblance to the adder's-tongue fern, *Ophioglossum* sp., which has a solitary leaf.

Description: This graceful species usually has one flower perched atop a slender six- to twelve-inch stem. A single narrow leaf occurs about midway up the stem. Infrequently, there are two flowers (very rarely three) on a single stem, each opening in succession from the lower to upper position.

The size of the three sepals and two petals of the one-inch-wide flowers is approximately equal. The lip projects forward and is covered with fleshy protuberances resembling thick hairs. The color of the sepals and petals is generally some shade of pink (rarely white), while the lip is deep purplish magenta on the tip and edges, with a bright yellow center.

In flower: May to July.

Habitat: Open bogs, seepages, damp meadows, and ditches.

Range: This is generally a coastal plain orchid but is occasionally found in the mountains and piedmont.

Pollinators: Bees.

This is one of my favorite orchids. It is often found growing among species of *Calopogon* (grass-pink orchids) since they both prefer damp or boggy environments. The group that I visit every year grows in the upstate in a seepage next to a pond. I find them within six inches of the water's edge. When I photographed the group below, I was standing in about one foot of water.

A showy group of rose pogonia in their springtime finery.

Often, these orchids can be found in large groups of 100 or more plants. When they are mixed in with magenta-colored grass-pink orchids *(Calopogon tuberosus)*, deep red sundews *(Drosera rotundifolia)*, and vivid yellow horned bladderworts *(Utricularia cornuta)*, it is a beautiful sight. Sometimes, though, I wish they would point their flowers in the same direction (much better for photography). However, I am thankful just for the opportunity to visit these graceful beauties each spring.

The flower resembles what most people would associate with a typical orchid. It has spreading sepals and forward-pointing petals of approximately equal length, and the lip has a shape that is a powerful attractor for insects, especially for naive bees. Since the flower does not provide a nectar reward, pollination depends on inexperienced bees. Once the bee visits a few flowers and receives no payback in the form of either nectar or pollen, it will generally find a more suitable species to visit. There must be a large supply of these naive bees since almost all of the plants I have seen, produce plentiful seed each season.

As the descriptive text mentions, occasionally one is fortunate enough to find a *Pogonia ophioglossoides* stem with two flowers as is pictured below right, or even one with three flowers. Oddly, some populations in the southern states appear to have quite a few two-flowered stems, while others do not. Consider yourself even more fortunate if you find a white-flowered *P. ophioglossoides*. This is a truly rare occurrence.

Rare white-flowered rose pogonia.

Unusual two-flowered rose pogonia.

NOTES:

Shadow-witch Orchid
Ponthieu's Orchid

Ponthieva racemosa (Walter) Mohr

Genus: Ponthieva—Named for the French botanist Henri de Ponthieu, who collected plants in the Caribbean, where he most likely saw this species.

Species epithet: racemosa—From Latin, meaning "raceme," which describes the grouping of flowers on the stem.

Description: The half-inch green and white flowers, downy reddish brown stem, and large, flat, green basal rosette of leaves makes this species easy to identify. Often, it is found in large groups growing in damp woods or along stream banks in the coastal plain. The five-inch leaves and one- to two-foot stem support up to twenty flowers that open sequentially from the bottom to the top.

The flower is white with green stripes and is nonresupinate (lip positioned uppermost). The only other species in South Carolina that have nonresupinate flowers are several species of *Calopogon* and *Gymnadeniopsis nivea.*

In flower: September through October.

Habitat: Calcium-rich soils along stream banks and damp woods.

Range: Along the coast and coastal plain.

Pollinators: Small insects.

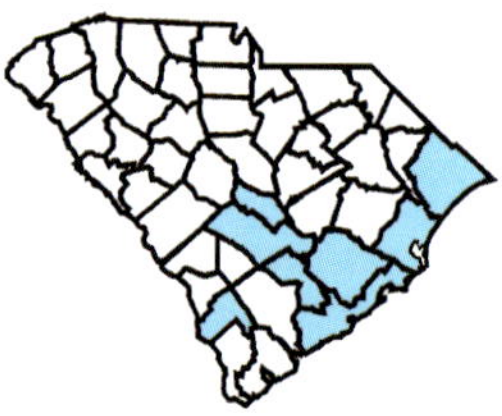

It's always fun to search the creek banks in the lowcountry looking for orchids. You never know what you are going to find. This peculiar looking orchid is often found growing with the club-spur orchid *(Gymnadeniopsis clavellata),* fragrant ladies'-tresses *(Spiranthes odorata),* and Florida adder's-mouth orchid *(Malaxis spicata).* Of course, not all bloom at the same time. In fact, the club-spur orchid is usually in seed when the shadow-witch orchid reaches full bloom.

Cluster of about twenty flowers and buds on a single stem.

Once, while looking for the shadow-witch orchid along a shaded creek bank, I found myself standing in the middle of a large group of them; most had been hidden by tall reeds and other undergrowth. I had to be very careful not to step on any other plants as I positioned myself along their edge.

It was early in their bloom season, but upon close inspection, I was able to find a single plant in bloom with two open flowers. It would be a couple of weeks before the other hundreds of plants would put on a glorious display in the shady woods.

To my knowledge, this is the only orchid species in the state that places its flowers horizontally, with the flower pointing up toward the sky. The nonresupinate flowers are supported on the stem by a relatively long pedicel, which makes them look like tiny hands held out for close inspection. It is a pleasure to find this orchid in flower. Their occurrence in large groups, their light green basal rosette of leaves, and showy green and white flowers on stout stems are just a few reasons to look for this species when it is in season.

A large group of shadow-witch orchids just coming into bloom in the damp woods near a stream.

NOTES:

Spiked Medusa
Crestless Plume Orchid

Pteroglossaspis ecristata (Fernald) Rolfe

Genus: Pteroglossaspis—From three Greek words: "ptron," meaning wing, "glossa," meaning tongue, and "aspis," meaning shield.

Species epithet: ecristata—From Latin, meaning "without a crest." *Pteroglossaspis* was often included in the genus *Eulophia* and was the only species in this genus whose lip had no crest.

Description: This strange looking orchid attains a height of up to four feet. It sends up a single stem, which rises out of the ground separate from its two or three pleated, grasslike leaves. The leaves are generally about two feet long. At the tip of the long stem is a small cluster of twisted flowers.

The four to twelve flowers on a single stem are about one-half inch wide and are generally some shade of greenish brown or bronze. The lip is dark purple or mahogany.

In flower: June to September.

Habitat: Pine savannahs, fields, and dry grassy clearings.

Range: Uncommon; mostly along the inner coastal plain.

Pollinators: Self-pollinating.

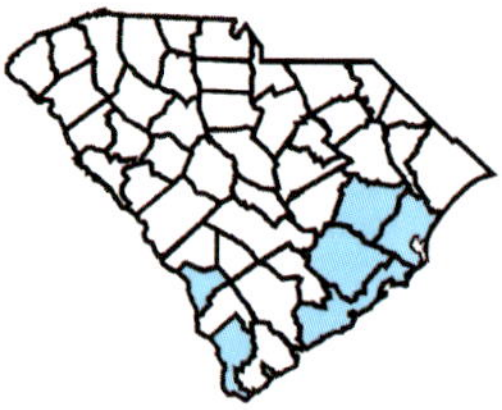

Pteroglossaspis ecristata is difficult to see in the wild. More than once, I have almost stepped on one of these orchid plants not realizing that I was so close. Its habit of growing in fields and savannahs that also support tall grasses and other such plants, lends to its excellent camouflage. One technique that I use to successfully spot them in the field is to squat down so that my head is about three feet from the ground, then I look around for plants growing at about eye level.

Two lanceolate leaves growing apart from the flowering stem to the right.

In my opinion, this orchid's bloom is quite peculiar. It does not fully open, so that it looks like it is in a continual bud stage. In addition, the flowers seem to be curiously curved around the stem rather than pointing out or up as is seen in other orchid species.

It was once thought to be quite rare in the state. But recent periodic prescribed burns have resulted in more sightings of these strangely beautiful orchids. More than a few of the state's orchid species seem to have a strict requirement for a lack of vegetative competition. This species appears to stay in a semidormant state until conditions are appropriate for it to send its leaves and stem above the surrounding foliage.

If you get a chance to see this orchid in flower, you will understand why a picture does not do it justice. It is difficult to capture the vertical posture of a plant whose flowers appear only on the top couple of inches of the three to four-foot stem. In addition, there seems to be no way to crane your neck to get a good view of the inside of the flower. Only when positioned under the bloom and looking up might you be lucky enough to catch its essence.

This is probably our most mysterious orchid. Take the time to search it out and study it closely, and you will be richly rewarded.

A group of seed pods with the dried flowers still attached—late August.

NOTES:

Spiranthes

By far, the most difficult part of writing this book was dealing with the befuddling, subtle differences among several of the species in the genus *Spiranthes*, commonly known as the ladies'-tresses orchids. When species designation must consider the size of the lip's basal tuberosities, the relative length of the flower bract, the variability of lip constriction, the shape of the inflorescence, the degree and type of pubescence, whether the leaves are present or absent at blooming, the extent to which the lateral sepals are reflexed, whether the seeds are monoembryonic or polyembryonic, et cetera, it is easy to understand why many of the most grounded experts in the field scratch their collective heads when trying to differentiate the species.

Although there are more than a dozen *Spiranthes* species in South Carolina, the four species that present the most difficulty are *S. cernua, S. ochroleuca, S. odorata,* and *S. magnicamporum* (a more western species that has not been reported in the state). *Spiranthes ochroleuca*, *S. odorata*, and *S. magnicamporum* were all originally described as individual species. But in 1950, Correll treated *S. odorata* and *S. ochroleuca* as varieties of the widespread and highly variable *S. cernua*. Subsequently, Sheviak, in 1982, following his publication on *S. magnicamporum*, restored both *S. odorata* and *S. ochroleuca* to species status. He makes this conclusion because *S. cernua* is a complex species with genes from many different related species within its origins (a compilospecies) and because it occurs in very distinctive regional races. For these reasons, although the position of the flowers (nodding) does not vary, *S. cernua* does not always look exactly the same in every area. This variability often can be confusing, but it is important to understand that among North American ladies'-tresses, this characteristic is unique to *S. cernua*.

Having said this, I continue to find this genus quite intriguing. Superficially, all the *Spiranthes* species look quite similar, having white flowers spiraling at the top of a thin green stem. Some spirals are loose and singular, appearing as a single row of flowers winding up the stem like a spiral staircase. Other spirals are so tight that they look like several columns of flowers on a stem. In some plants, these columns are aligned and appear to be completely vertical.

Most of the *Spiranthes* species produce flowers that have very little or no fragrance. However, one South Carolina species is quite fragrant. It is aptly named *S. odorata.* Its strong fragrance is a main characteristic that helps differentiate it from other species. Generally, it is a coastal plain species that is found from Virginia to Texas.

Spiranthes flower size varies considerably. In *S. odorata*, the flowers are up to one-half inch long, while *S. tuberosa* and *S. lacera* var. *gracilis* produce flowers one-eighth inch long or less. Take it from me, these tiny flowers are very hard to spot, especially when the plant is growing among tall grasses.

As I have previously indicated, the flower color of the state's *Spiranthes* species is basically white. I say "basically" since, from a distance, all the *Spiranthes* species appear to produce white flowers. Upon closer examination (much closer for the smaller flowers), there is quite a variety of color, especially in the lip. For example, the lip of *S. lacera* var. *gracilis* has a definite green blotch in the center. The lip of *S. praecox* is white with green veins radiating from the base of the lip. The lip of *S. ochroleuca* has a creamy yellow or butterscotch stripe down the center. Still, for the most part, all the other flower parts are pure white.

Whether you are interested in closely studying the species of this wonderfully complex genus, or just appreciating their delicate beauty from a distance, I think you will find great satisfaction simply from being in their presence.

Nodding Ladies'-tresses

Spiranthes cernua (Linnaeus) L. C. Richard

Genus: Spiranthes—From Greek, meaning "coiled" or "spiraled," referring to the spiral pattern of flowers on the stem.

Species epithet: cernua—From Latin, meaning "inclining the head," or "nodding."

Description: The bright white, sometimes lightly-fragrant flowers of this species are about one-quarter to one-half inch long. The flowers, which are generally aligned on the stem in ranks of loose spirals or straight lines, are curved downward ("nodding"). The inner portion of the lip is a pale, creamy white, while the outer part of the lip is translucent. The bloom stem is from six to twelve or more inches tall and is covered with tiny blunt hairs. The inflorescence takes on a thin cylindrical shape when all of the flowers are open.

A basal rosette of long narrow leaves may be present or absent at blooming. This plant is commonly seen in large groups.

This species prefers damp or wet growing conditions and is often found in bright sun.

In flower: Late August through November.

Habitat: In moist grassy fields, wet meadows, and damp roadside ditches.

Range: Scattered locations over all of the state.

Pollinators: Self-pollinating.

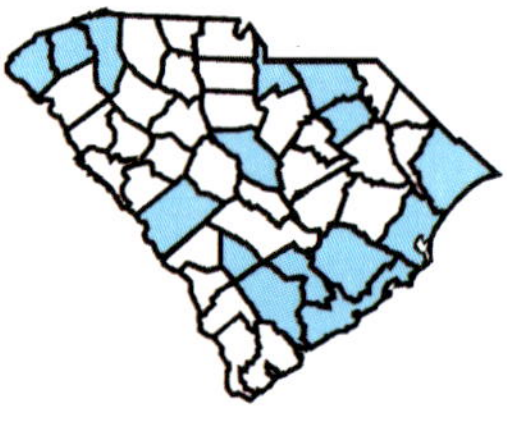

In general, *Spiranthes cernua* orchids are found in a variety of habitats. I have seen them growing on a damp hillside where they get most of the hill's runoff as well as in wet ditches and along pond margins. In all cases, they like to have their feet close to water.

Slender, graceful spiral of flowers.

The tall graceful spirals of pure white flowers, sometimes two feet tall, shine brightly against the dark green background of a ditch bank. Many times, there are hundreds of plants in an area covering just a few square feet—a beautiful sight.

Besides setting seeds, this species can propagate via stolons or underground runners, allowing it to freely multiply in large numbers.

When in bloom, some plants have lower leaves that can be up to six inches long, while on other plants, the leaves will have withered at bloom time. In most cases, there are several small bractlike leaves that appear every couple of inches from the base of the stem to just below where the flowers begin.

The flowers usually appear in three or four ranks, or rows. Sometimes the flowers of one plant appear to twist up the stem, while another plant will have flowers that are in straight vertical rows.

This is one of the latest orchids to bloom in the state, often staying in flower well into November. Sometimes, it can be found growing beside the water-spider orchid *(Habenaria repens)*. They both like very wet conditions.

Every year as the leaves are beginning to turn and as the days begin to get a little cooler, I look forward to seeing this beautiful orchid. It is a favorite of mine and one that I can count on to provide loads of blossoms every year.

Small group of nodding ladies'-tresses growing in a wet pond margin.

NOTES:

Eaton's Ladies'-tresses

Spiranthes eatonii Ames ex P. M. Brown

Genus: Spiranthes—From Greek, meaning "coiled" or "spiraled," referring to the spiral pattern of flowers on the stem.

Species epithet: eatonii—Named for A. A. Eaton, a botanist who collected the first specimens of this species in 1905 in south Florida.

Description: The tiny flowers of this species are only about one-sixth inch in length and have a somewhat tubular appearance. It can be distinguished from other similar species, which are also bright white and have a green spot on the lip, by its date of blooming (April to May) and by its geographic location (strictly in the coastal plain). The petals are rounded but not incurved and are green at the base. The thin, loosely coiled flowering stem is about twelve to twenty inches tall. Oblanceolate basal leaves, which can reach two inches in length, are sometimes present at blooming.

In flower: April to May.

Habitat: In grassy fields, roadsides, and dry to damp open pine flatwoods.

Range: Strictly in the coastal plain.

Pollinators: Perhaps small bees or wasps.

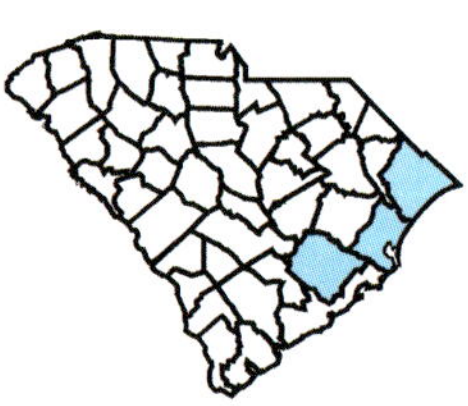

I describe this species as tall and gangly. And, if the wind is stirring, it is very difficult to photograph. The stems are so thin and long that the slightest breeze causes the inflorescence to swing back and forth like the pendulum on a clock.

However, it is easy to say good things about this bright white *Spiranthes*. Although the flowers are somewhat diminutive, the green-spotted lip is crisp, and the flowers are relatively long and tubular. The loose spiral often gives many of the flowers the appearance of being in a single vertical column. For photography, this is great, since many of the flowers align themselves along the same vertical plane.

Also, it is nice that this basal-leaved *Spiranthes* sometimes keeps its leaves, even at bloom time, although many of the leaves often appear to be partially eaten by insects. This is not unusual for leaves that lie on the ground.

Close-up of the basal rosette of the oblanceolate leaves of Spiranthes eatonii.

The last time I saw and photographed this species was when I found them growing at the edge of a cemetery in the woods. I don't know why some *Spiranthes* species prefer this habitat. My guess is that the ground is frequently disturbed, and like other plants it prefers the conditions of disturbed areas. Fortunately, these locations are usually kept free of competing plants, so the *Spiranthes* do quite well during their short blooming season.

Spiranthes eatonii is found in a number of locations scattered along the coastal plain. Although it has been reported only from Berkeley, Georgetown, and Horry Counties, it is likely that it will be found in Charleston, Beaufort, and the other coastal plain counties. Wherever you might find this species, its presentation and bright coloration will impress you.

Close-up showing the narrow, tubular flowers characteristic of Spiranthes eatonii.

NOTES:

Florida Ladies'-tresses

Spiranthes floridana (Wherry) Cory emend. P. M. Brown

Genus: *Spiranthes*—From Greek, meaning "coiled" or "spiraled," referring to the spiral pattern of flowers on the stem.

Species epithet: *floridana*—Named for the state of Florida, where it was first found and described.

Description: This species can be easily confused with another species, *Spiranthes brevilabris* (the short-lipped ladies'-tresses), which has not yet been found in the state. Close examination of the flowers and stem helps distinguish *S. floridana* from *S. brevilabris.* The latter is densely pubescent while the former is glabrous, or without pubescence.

Otherwise, the two species share many other characteristics: yellow green leaves that are withered at flowering time, creamy yellow flowers, a lip with a yellow center, and a single rank of flowers in a loose spiral.

In flower: April to May.

Habitat: In grassy fields, roadsides, and dry to damp open pine flatwoods.

Range: Strictly in the coastal plain.

Pollinators: Perhaps mosquitoes.

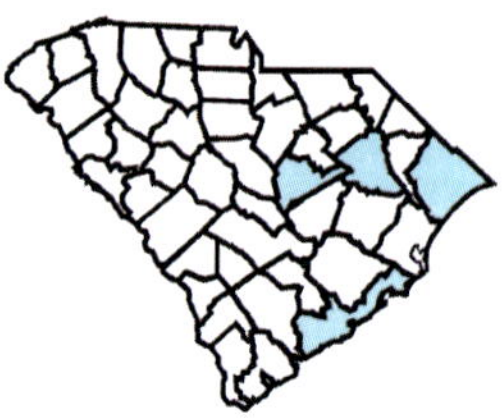

It's quite satisfying to find a scarce orchid species growing in an area that is protected by a corporation with an interest in conservation. When I first saw this species, it was growing in the front yard of the headquarters of a forest products company. The administrators are aware that this delicate species grows wild just outside of their office window and have vowed to protect it.

As the bloom stems begin to sprout in late winter and early spring, the basal rosette of leaves begins to wither. These leaves are often absent when the plant is in full bloom. The leaves are yellow green in color and are horizontal to the ground's surface. When the leaves are present, they are quite well hidden among the grasses.

Close-up of the basal rosette of the oblanceolate leaves of Spiranthes floridana.

The flowers are a creamy yellow or ivory color with a yellow blotch on the center of the lip. The base, where the petals and sepals join the ovary, is green. Both the flowers and the stem are without pubescence. This is a distinguishing characteristic that separates it from its close cousin, the short-lipped ladies'-tresses *(Spiranthes brevilabris)*, which is densely pubescent. It has yet to be found in the state, and grows much further south in Georgia, Florida, and Texas.

This orchid that will not catch your eye as you speed down the highway, but you might find it if you look carefully along roadsides and in damp meadows.

Close-up showing the green base of the petals and sepals. Also, note the absence of hairs on the stem and flower parts. The absence of hairs is a defining characteristic that separates this species from the similar and rare Spiranthes brevilabris, *which is not found in South Carolina.*

NOTES:

Southern Slender Ladies'-tresses

Spiranthes lacera (Rafinesque) Rafinesque var. *gracilis* (Bigelow) Luer

Genus: *Spiranthes*—From Greek, meaning "coiled" or "spiraled," referring to the spiral pattern of flowers on the stem.

Species epithet: *lacera* var. *gracilis*—From Latin referring to the "cutting" or "laceration" on the edge of the lip, and "graceful."

Description: The tiny flowers of this species are only about one-eighth inch long. The pearly white flower can be differentiated from similar species by the green spot on the lip, which has a white edge or margin. The petals are rounded and incurved. The flower stem is about twelve to eighteen inches tall. There are no leaves present at blooming.

In flower: Mid-June to mid-July.

Habitat: In grassy fields, roadsides, and the margins of forests containing moist to dry acidic soil.

Range: Generally in the northwestern counties but also scattered in the coastal plain. Another similar variety *(S. lacera* var. *lacera)* exists in the northern United States, but it keeps its leaves at bloom time.

Pollinators: Flies and small bees.

This orchid's graceful spiral of flowers are so tiny and delicate that they give me an impression of my grandmother's tatting or of a spiral of fine lace. Although the flowers are bright white, they are extremely difficult to spot, especially in tall grasses.

The stem pictured below was growing in tall grasses just a few feet off the highway. Actually, I did not spot it; my traveling companion did. I was busy looking at the green adder's-mouth orchids *(Malaxis unifolia)* and the yellow fringed orchids *(Platanthera ciliaris)* that were growing less than a foot away—a very nice roadside site.

Actual size of inflorescence.

A close look at the stem of this orchid will make a person incredulous that such a thin stem could hold flowers almost fifteen inches off the ground. The picture to the left shows the actual size of this delicate orchid with its one-eighth-inch-long flowers.

Many *Spiranthes* are difficult to identify. However, this one, with the green spot on its lip and its diminutive size, is easy to identify. The lack of leaves when the plant is in flower is another defining characteristic. The northern variety of this species, *S. lacera* var. *lacera*, has several basal leaves present when it is blooming, whereas *S. lacera* var. *gracilis*, the southern variety, does not.

Although this species can be found in scattered counties over the entire state, the ones pictured here were found in the upper reaches of Oconee County.

While photographing these plants, I was lucky enough to witness a small sweat fly visiting the flowers, from the lowermost to the topmost on the stem. Bumblebees are the known pollinators of this species, but there is proof that other insects visit as well.

Finding this graceful orchid amid the tall grasses growing alongside a busy highway is a special bonus for anyone with the time to look for these treasures. But don't expect to see it while driving. You will have to walk the roadside ditches to find this elusive orchid.

Sweat fly, up close and personal, pollinating this tiny orchid.

NOTES:

Lace-lipped Ladies'-tresses

Spiranthes laciniata (Small) Ames

Genus: Spiranthes—From Greek, meaning "coiled" or "spiraled," referring to the spiral pattern of flowers on the stem.

Species epithet: laciniata—From Latin, meaning "deeply cut," referring to the ragged incisions on the edges of the lip.

Description: The three-eighth-inch flowers of this species are quite similar to the early blooming species, *Spiranthes vernalis* (spring ladies'-tresses). The main difference is the pubescence. *Spiranthes vernalis* has acuminate or pointed hairs, and *S. laciniata* has capitate or ball-tipped hairs. The plant is one to two feet tall when in flower. The flowers are arranged in a very loose spiral or are sometimes secund. They are creamy white to ivory with a yellow center on the lip. The lip is finely lacerated along the edge, giving it a lacelike appearance. There are three to five grasslike leaves present at blooming.

In flower: June to July.

Habitat: Wet grassy fields and wet roadside ditches.

Range: Generally along the coastal plain.

Pollinators: Flies and bumblebees.

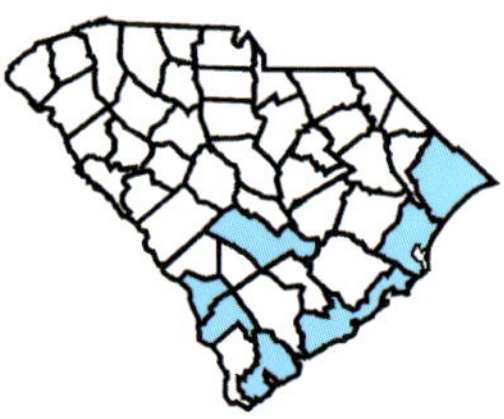

When I found the plants photographed in this chapter, they were growing in a wet ditch among a number of snowy orchid *(Gymnadeniopsis nivea)* plants. The flowers closely resemble the flowers of the spring ladies'-tresses *(Spiranthes vernalis)*. However, when I spotted them, I knew that they could also be the scarcer species, lace-lipped ladies'-tresses *(S. laciniata)*.

These Spiranthes laciniata *flowers closely resemble those of the species* Spiranthes vernalis.

Since both species are late spring or early summer bloomers, they were the most likely candidates. I knew that there was one sure way to tell them apart. I needed to examine the pubescence, or small hairs, that grow on the stem and flowers. If the pubescence was acuminate, or pointed, then it would have to be *S. vernalis*. It is the only *Spiranthes* species with pointed hairs. If the pubescence was ball-tipped, then it was most likely *S. laciniata*.

The pubescence turned out to be ball-tipped, and thus, what I was looking at was lace-lipped ladies'-tresses. I was pleased to find these orchids, since they are quite scarce in the state.

Although the lip color is approximately the same in both species, the lip of the lace-lipped ladies'-tresses is a bit more blunt and does not extend down and fold under as does the lip of the spring ladies'-tresses. Also, the lace-lipped ladies'-tresses tends to bloom a few weeks later than its cousin.

Spiranthes laciniata tends not to grow in large groups as do some of South Carolina's other *Spiranthes* species, so don't expect to find big clumps of this hard-to-find plant. However, it is hardy and vigorous and can grow up to thirty inches tall.

After examining the photographs in this chapter, you can see how *S. laciniata* is easily mistaken for another species. This illustrates the importance of taking a hand lens into the field. It not only magnifies even the smallest flowers, but it is also useful as a tool for distinguishing species.

A closer view showing the lacelike edges of the lip.

NOTES:

Long-lipped Ladies'-tresses

Spiranthes longilabris Lindley

Genus: Spiranthes—From Greek, meaning "coiled" or "spiraled," referring to the spiral pattern of flowers on the stem.

Species epithet: longilabris—From two Latin words meaning "long" and "lip," referring to the proportions of the lip.

Description: The quarter-inch flowers of this species are easy to identify. They appear as a tight single rank or are sometimes secund. The plant ranges from one foot to about two feet tall when in flower. The flowers are white with a creamy yellow center and are marked with a touch of green on the inside of the lip. The lateral sepals are spread widely, while the broad lip is oblong and tends to curl slightly under at the tip. The fact that this species blooms rather late in the year helps separate it from two similar species, *S. laciniata* and *S. vernalis.*

The thin, narrow leaves are generally withered at blooming.

In flower: Late October to early November.

Habitat: Damp, grassy longleaf pine savannahs and moist, grassy meadows.

Range: Rare. Reported from two counties in the coastal plain.

Pollinators: Certain moths and bees.

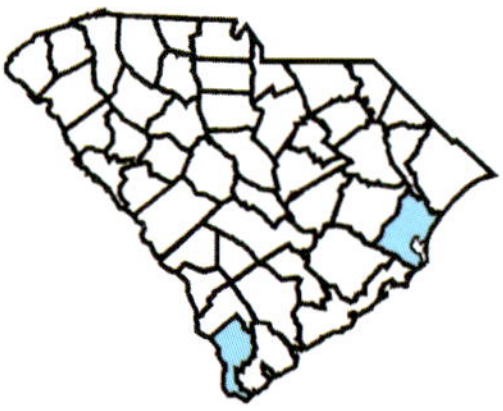

Spiranthes longilabris is one of the rarest *Spiranthes* in the state. According to my research, it has not been reported in the state since 1972. It is believed to still grow in South Carolina, but since it has been found only on posted, private hunting preserves, it is difficult to determine its true status.

Note how the lateral sepals spread widely from the lip and petals.

I managed to photograph this scarce species in the Green Swamp of North Carolina. The Green Swamp is a 16,000-acre coastal plain preserve that is owned, managed, and protected by the Nature Conservancy. Its plant diversity is similar to South Carolina's Francis Marion National Forest, which provides habitat for many of the orchid species found in this book.

Many consider *Spiranthes longilabris* as the most beautiful of the North American *Spiranthes*. Its white flowers show a splash of yellow or green in the center of the lip, making it a colorful surprise in the tall wire grass *(Aristida stricta)* of the savannah. The remarkable feature that sets it apart from most of South Carolina's other *Spiranthes* species is the tremendous spread of its lateral sepals. Sometimes, it looks as though each flower is trying to fly away from its moorings.

The flowers lie in a very loose spiral around the stem. Often, the flowers are secund, meaning they appear only on one side of the stem, as in the photo above. As I mentioned previously, the stem is not tall, attaining a length of around twelve inches. For this reason, it is very difficult to spot in its tall grassy surroundings. Diligent effort is necessary to find these lovely plants.

Spiranthes longilabris is one of the last fall *Spiranthes* to bloom in its habitat. Close by, you can usually find fragrant ladies'-tresses *(S. odorata)*, a very robust

Large inflorescence just beginning to bloom in a longleaf pine savannah.

NOTES:

and fragrant orchid that is common in the swampy lowlands of the state. Both *S. longilabris* and *S. odorata* are in peak bloom in October and early November.

If you manage to locate a population of *S. longilabris* or any of the state's other rare plant species, it would be a good idea to notify the state botanist with the South Carolina Department of Natural Resources, especially if the population is on state or federal lands. This way, you can do your part to help protect what is quickly becoming a scarce species.

Yellow Ladies'-tresses

Spiranthes ochroleuca (Rydberg) Rydberg

Genus: Spiranthes—From Greek, meaning "coiled" or "spiraled," referring to the spiral pattern of flowers on the stem.

Species epithet: ochroleuca—From two Latin words: "ochro," meaning "pale," and "leuca" meaning "white."

Description: The flowers of this species are usually more yellowish than its close cousin *Spiranthes cernua,* which has bright white flowers. The underside of the lip is usually a shade of butterscotch. The flowers either point horizontal or slightly upward and are definitely not "nodding," like those of *S. cernua.*

The bloom stem is about ten to fifteen inches tall and is usually tightly coiled. The three to five slender, acuminate basal leaves are present at blooming.

This species is generally considered to have a more northerly distribution in North America. The single site where it is found in South Carolina may represent its most southern location.

In flower: Late September to mid-October.

Habitat: Rather dry ditch banks, fields, and forest edges.

Range: Rare. Currently, only a single site in Oconee County.

Pollinators: Small bees.

Spiranthes ochroleuca is not commonly found in South Carolina. In fact, in my search of the state's herbaria, I have seen only a single vouchered specimen. The dried specimen was originally identified as nodding ladies'-tresses *(Spiranthes cernua)*, but an expert on the genus *Spiranthes* subsequently re-identified it as *S. ochroleuca*.

Notice the hump in the dorsal sepal of the lower flowers and the straight lateral sepals.

It was this single specimen that led me on the search for living plants within the boundaries of the state. The voucher specimen was collected in 1983 from the ledge of an old rock quarry in Oconee County. A couple of decades is a long time in the life of an orchid colony; moreover, I doubted whether I could even locate the site.

Armed with a topographic map of the area, a compass, and a bottle of bug spray for protection against chiggers, I set off to find this elusive orchid. After walking a couple of miles on a logging road and then scrambling down a heavily wooded mountainside, I actually saw the outline of an old rock quarry. It was so overgrown that it was hardly recognizable. Large trees were growing among huge boulders in its center.

After carefully searching the area, I saw the narrow, twelve-foot-high ledge mentioned in the voucher documentation. I somehow managed to scramble up on the narrow ledge. Immediately, I saw about a dozen *Spiranthes* growing in the loose debris littered in the cracks and crevices between the rocks. Unsure that this was *S. ochroleuca*, I quickly inspected the underside of the flower and saw that it had a definite butterscotch color, which is a distinguishing characteristic for this species. The flowers also exhibited a hump along the dorsal portion, but the flower did not nod. The lateral sepals were held close in to the lip and pointed straight out. I had finally found the single location listed in the state for this elusive plant.

Close-up view from beneath the flower, showing the butterscotch color of the underside of the lip.

Now, my only problem was figuring out how to get down from the ledge and to get myself back to my car in one piece. Obviously, I made it back, but I would not encourage anyone to recreate this particular experience, since it was very dangerous. I could have been in serious trouble had I slipped on the narrow ledge.

I did, however, leave with the knowledge that *S. ochroleuca* still lives in the state. I expect that there may be even more populations hidden away in little known locations, perhaps similar to the one I visited.

Fragrant Ladies'-tresses

Spiranthes odorata (Nuttall) Lindley

Genus: Spiranthes—From Greek, meaning "coiled" or "spiraled," referring to the spiral pattern of flowers on the stem.

Species epithet: odorata—From Latin, meaning "scented" or "perfumed," referring to the strong scent of the flowers.

Description: Spiranthes odorata has the largest flowers of all the state's *Spiranthes* species. The strongly fragrant flowers reach a length of one-half inch or greater. The fragrance is similar to that of vanilla, cumarin, or jasmine. Each flower is white with a lip whose center is usually a creamy yellow but may also be greenish yellow. The flowers are configured in a tight coil, which usually results in three ranks, or columns, which may be entirely vertical or slightly twisted. The plants may attain a height of almost three feet but are usually one to two feet high.

The broad leaves, which are present at blooming, are up to one foot long and are relatively thick. They appear as a basal rosette, but smaller bractlike leaves clasp about half the length of the stem.

This species reproduces by seeds and by stolons.

In flower: October to early November.

Habitat: Moist roadside ditches, cypress swamps, pine flatwoods, and the edges of creeks and rivers in dense shade.

Range: Widely scattered in the sandhills and coastal plain.

Pollinators: Certain moths and bees.

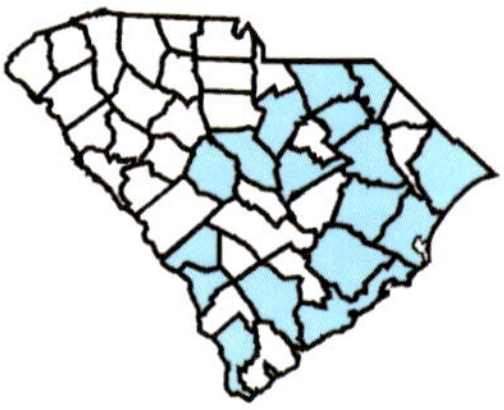

In the process of searching for the many lovely orchid species found in the state, I find myself from time to time mired knee-deep in swamp mud or tripping over cypress knees and roots hidden under leaf litter. It is the nature of the task.

Some of the state's orchids prefer habitats that see more snakes and alligators on a daily basis than they see people. *Spiranthes odorata* is no exception. This orchid species is a robust plant with strongly fragrant white flowers. Often, this fragrance can be detected from a dozen feet away. Sometimes you smell the fragrance before you actually see the flowers. Some liken the fragrance to vanilla, but I think it has a more earthy quality.

Showy raceme of tightly packed, large, and fragrant flowers.

Each inflorescence is usually composed of twelve to sixty or more pubescent white flowers. Though most parts of the flower are a bright white, the central portion of the lip may be cream, yellow, or greenish yellow.

The flowers are configured in a tight coil, which usually results in three vertical ranks. These ranks may appear to be perfectly vertical or may seem to be slightly twisted. When the plant is in full bloom, the inflorescence takes on the shape of a long cylinder.

The broad basal leaves of *S. odorata* are quite large compared to other *Spiranthes* species. They may reach a foot or more in length and are relatively thick and straplike.

Although you may see single plants scattered about, you more likely will see clumps or groups of plants due to

It is common to find Spiranthes odorata *in large clumps. Note the large number of sprouting immature plants that are the result of numerous stolons from the parent plants.*

the stoloniferous nature of its reproduction; the plants send out stolons as far as several feet away that will eventually become new plants.

Considering that orchids grow in some very unusual places, I find it refreshing to see the beautiful flowers and to detect the delicate fragrance of *S. odorata* in the midst of boot-sucking mud and decaying vegetation.

NOTES:

Northern Oval Ladies'-tresses

Spiranthes ovalis Lindley var. *erostellata* Catling

Genus: Spiranthes—From Greek, meaning "coiled" or "spiraled," referring to the spiral pattern of flowers on the stem.

Species epithet: ovalis var. *erostellata*—From Latin, meaning "oval," referring to the general shape of the inflorescence, and "without a rostellum," which is an extension from the upper edge of the stigma.

Description: The quarter-inch flowers of this species are usually grouped tightly at the top of an eight- to ten-inch stem. The inflorescence usually has from twenty to forty flowers.

The plants thrive in the habitat of the deep woods. Each plant is pubescent and usually has three or four shiny, narrow leaves on the lower half of the stem. The leaves are present at flowering.

Most of the oval ladies'-tresses found in the southeastern U.S. belong to the variety *erostellata,* whose small flowers form in three fairly vertical ranks. The flowers appear to be cleistogamous, or closed, but always reproduce quite well. The ovaries swell with seeds even as the plant blooms. This happens because the flower is missing some of the reproductive parts necessary for pollination by insects, but is self-pollinating.

In flower: Mid-September to October.

Habitat: Moist to dry undisturbed woods.

Range: Widely scattered in many locations in the state.

Pollinators: Self-pollinating.

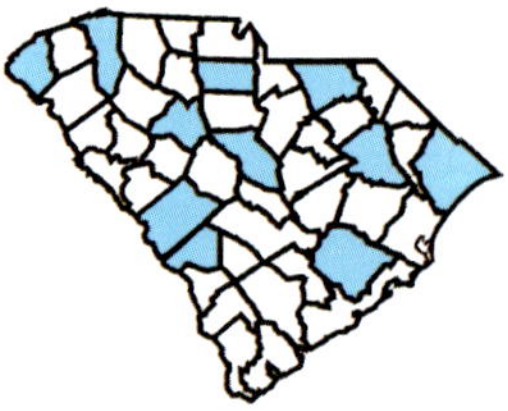

As my companions and I were heading toward the deep woods at the end of an old farm road, we saw a stem or two of white flowers sticking up through the heavy grass in the middle of the wet road. Upon close inspection, we determined that they were definitely a *Spiranthes*, but it happened to be nodding ladies'-tresses *(Spiranthes cernua)* and not the species we were looking for. We didn't expect to find *S. ovalis* var. *erostellata* in the middle of a sunny road anyway. It prefers a heavily shaded habitat.

Note the tightly coiled inflorescence and the flowers, which never fully open. Also, note the fullness of the ovaries that are already expanding with seed.

Soon we came to a stream that crossed the road. We immediately turned to enter the adjacent woods. Almost at once, we saw three or four fairly short plants with white inflorescences. This was what we had come to see.

The flowers, which appeared in three distinct ranks, or vertical columns, were tightly coiled on the topmost fifth of the stem. When we looked closer, we saw that none of the flowers appeared fully open, yet the ovaries were already expanding as if they had been pollinated weeks before. This is a defining characteristic of *S. ovalis* var. *erostellata.*

Since it is missing one of the essential flower parts necessary for pollination by insects, the rostellum, it self-pollinates, which explains why the ovaries were expanded. Occasionally, plants with flowers that open more fully can be found. But they, too, are self-pollinating and lack the requisite rostellum.

Although its flowers are not the showiest of the state's *Spiranthes* species, *S. ovalis* var. *erostellata* has traits that make it worth looking for. Keep in mind that it is one of the shorter *Spiranthes*, and it prefers to grow in the deep woods where it is difficult to spot. Step carefully, it is easy to overlook.

The three or four leaves of Spiranthes ovalis *var.* erostellata *grow from the base to about halfway up the stem.*

NOTES:

Grass-leaved Ladies'-tresses

Spiranthes praecox (Walter) S. Watson

Genus: Spiranthes—From Greek, meaning "coiled" or "spiraled," referring to the spiral pattern of flowers on the stem.

Species epithet: praecox—From Latin, meaning "early ripening," referring to the early season in which it blooms and matures.

Description: The flowers of this species are less than one-half inch long. The bright white color of the flower and appressed lateral sepals are characteristics used to distinguish it from the similar species, *Spiranthes sylvatica.*

The rounded, concave lip is white with light to dark green veins radiating from the center. On rare occasions, the lip stripes are yellow or entirely absent. Its preferred habitat is the sunny bank of a roadside ditch. The petals are rounded and straight. The bloom stem is about twelve to twenty inches tall and may be loosely or tightly coiled. The three to five slender, acuminate leaves are present at blooming.

In flower: May through June.

Habitat: Sunny meadows and roadside ditches.

Range: Mainly in the sandhills and along the coastal plain.

Pollinators: Small insects, possibly mosquitoes.

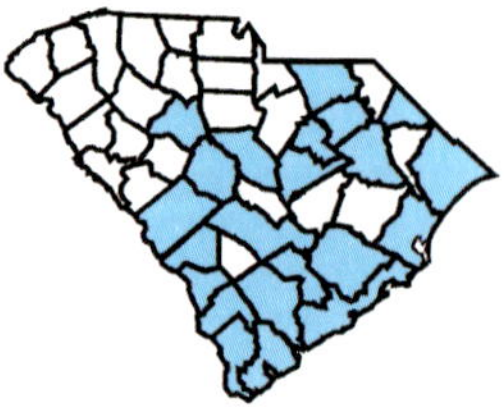

This species is easy to spot along the state's backroads, even if you are traveling at moderate speed. The bright white color of its flowers and its tendency to grow in clumps or small groups allows it to be seen quite readily.

The most outstanding feature of the flower is the appearance of the six to eight green stripes flowing out from the center of the lip. These stripes give the appearance of a delicate embroidery. Occasionally, however, you can find plants whose flowers either have very light yellow stripes or no stripes at all.

Loose spiral of tightly packed flowers. This is a white form with light yellow veins on the lip (forma albolabia*).*

Once, while photographing a huge drift of rose pogonia *(Pogonia ophioglossoides)* in a sunny roadside ditch, I noticed a cluster of white flowers just up the road. These flowers turned out to be a beautiful group of *Spiranthes praecox* in full bloom. They were just waiting to be photographed. The photograph I took that day appears on the previous page. It shows eight stems with perfectly shaped flowers. Each of these stems has flowers that are tightly coiled, but frequently, stems have flowers that are loosely coiled or are secund.

Since this species tends to bloom around the same time as several other *Spiranthes* species, it is a good idea to check the lip coloration to verify the identification of *S. praecox*. Even if the stripes are very faint or even missing, the bright white color and tubular shape of the flowers, the concave and rounded lip, and the presence of grassy leaves at bloom time should lead to the correct identification.

I always look forward to springtime when I can travel the secondary roads of the state and search the many beautiful ladies'-tresses orchids that are locally abundant. This species is one that is quite easy to find and will reward you with its delicate beauty.

Green veins on the lip and white petals and sepals are characteristics of Spiranthes praecox.

NOTES:

Woodland Ladies'-tresses

Spiranthes sylvatica P. M. Brown

Genus: Spiranthes—From Greek, meaning "coiled" or "spiraled," referring to the spiral pattern of flowers on the stem.

Species epithet: sylvatica—From Latin "sylva," meaning "woods," and the Latin suffix "atica," meaning "habitat."

Description: The flowers of this species are about one-half inch long. The creamy green color of the flower is a determining characteristic that distinguishes it from the similar species, *Spiranthes praecox*. The concave lip is pale green with darker green veins radiating from the center.

Its preferred habitat is in the shade of moist to dry woods. The petals are rounded and straight and appear to be connivent with the dorsal sepal. The bloom stem is about twelve to twenty inches tall and may be loosely or tightly coiled. The three to five slender, acuminate leaves are present at blooming.

In flower: May through June.

Habitat: Dry woods and shaded roadside banks.

Range: Strictly along the coastal plain.

Pollinators: Small insects, probably wasps.

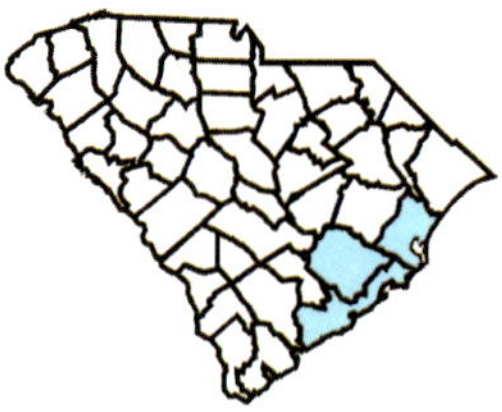

A walk in the deep woods is hardly where I expect to find *Spiranthes* growing in profusion. Most of the state's *Spiranthes* are found growing in full sun. However, this species thrives in dark, damp woods. If they are seen in a roadside habitat, they are found growing directly next to or under shrubby vegetation along a ditch bank, not out in the open.

When looking at the flowers up close, there is a superficial resemblance to *Spiranthes praecox*. In fact, *S. sylvatica* was formerly thought to be a shade-loving variant of *S. praecox*. Both have green veins on the oblong lip. But this is where the resemblance ends.

The inflorescence on the left is tightly coiled while the one on the right is very loosely coiled; both variations are equally common.

The flowers of *S. sylvatica* are gaping and are a creamy green color. *Spiranthes sylvatica* presents its flowers in both a loose spiral, a tight spiral, and all variations in between, while *S. praecox* normally presents its flowers in just a loose spiral. The flowers are found on the top quarter of the thin stem.

In recent years, many more *Spiranthes sylvatica* have been found and identified. So, when you are out in the dry woods of the coastal plain, be on the lookout for a creamy green *Spiranthes* growing in the shade.

Close-up showing the green stripes on the lip of Spiranthes sylvatica, *which also occur on* Spiranthes praecox.

NOTES:

Little Ladies'-tresses

Spiranthes tuberosa Rafinesque

Genus: *Spiranthes*—From Greek, meaning "coiled" or "spiraled," referring to the spiral pattern of flowers on the stem.

Species epithet: *tuberosa*—From Latin, meaning "tuberous," describing the distinctive tuberous root.

Description: The flowers of this species are about one-eighth inch long or less. The stem is one to two feet tall at bloom time. The petals, sepals, and lip are pure white. It is the only white midsummer blooming *Spiranthes* found in South Carolina.

Since it blooms at the same time as *Spiranthes lacera* var. *gracilis*, it might be confused with this species. However, its lip color is pure white—*S. lacera* var. *gracilis* sports a green blotch or stripe in its center. The basal rosette of oval leaves is withered by bloom time. The flowers are frequently seen in a loose spiral, but since this species is so variable, plants in the same population also may exhibit flowers in a tight spiral.

In flower: July to early August.

Habitat: Open pine forests, dry roadside ditches, and lawns.

Range: Widely scattered locations all over the state.

Pollinators: Small bees and other small insects.

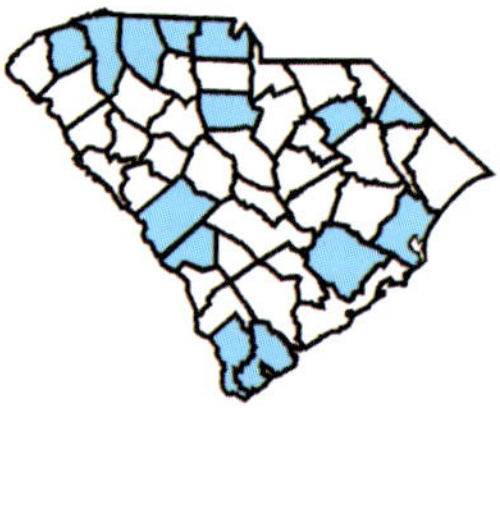

South Carolina has only two *Spiranthes* that bloom in the heat of midsummer: *Spiranthes lacera* var. *gracilis* and *S. tuberosa.* I might have mistaken the plants pictured in this chapter for the former had it not been for *S. tuberosa*'s pure white flowers showing brightly in the sunshine. *Spiranthes tubersosa* is the only pure white flowered summer-blooming *Spiranthes* in the state.

Tiny, iridescent green bee pollinating each of the flowers.

The flowers are exceedingly small, one-eighth inch long or less. The lip is finely ruffled along the edges, while the lateral sepals are separated from the rest of the flower by a narrow gap.

The flowers are arranged in various configurations on the stem. It is not unusual to find the flowers secund, or all on one side of the stem.

The tiny green bee pictured to the left is only about one-quarter inch long. It visited each and every flower on the stem, starting at the bottom and working its way to the topmost open flower. Conceivably, a single insect could pollinate a whole population of plants.

This species seems quite comfortable with city life. Often, it is found growing on a front lawn or in a ditch that is infrequently mowed. Although mowing helps eliminate tall-growing plants that would compete with the orchids for light, it is a two-edged sword. It is possible that the bloom stalk will be chopped off if the property is mowed too frequently.

If you are fortunate enough to find this delicate little orchid, be sure to use a magnifying glass so that you can appreciate all of its beauty. It is indeed a midsummer treat.

There is a dramatic difference between a very loose spiral (left) and a very tight spiral (right). These plants were from the same population and grew only a few feet apart.

NOTES:

Spring Ladies'-tresses

Spiranthes vernalis Engelmann & Gray

Genus: Spiranthes—From Greek, meaning "coiled" or "spiraled," referring to the spiral pattern of flowers on the stem.

Species epithet: vernalis—From Latin, meaning "of or belonging to spring," referring to the season when this species usually blooms in the southeast.

Description: The flowers of this species are about one-half inch long. The petals, sepals, and lip are white, but the center of the lip is thickened and is creamy yellow or ivory in color. Occasionally, the lip may have two orange or brown spots toward the apex. Each stem has as many as forty to fifty flowers, and the entire inflorescence is densely covered with articulated, pointed hairs. This characteristic distinguishes this species from the other *Spiranthes* species that grow in the state.

It is one of the earliest of the *Spiranthes* to bloom and generally keeps its leaves while blooming. The flowers are most often seen in a loose spiral, but since this characteristic varies, plants in the same population may exhibit flowers in a tight spiral.

In flower: April to June.

Habitat: Marshes, grassy banks, meadows, and roadside ditches.

Range: Scattered locations all over the state.

Pollinators: Small bees and other small insects.

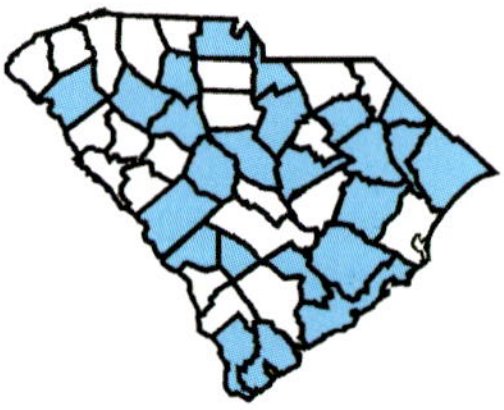

Serendipity often plays a big part in discovering new orchid locations. Late one spring, I rented a motel room while visiting one of my favorite orchid hunting areas in the lowcountry. I arrived late in the evening and did not have time to do anything but unpack and go to bed.

Loose spiral of flowers with orange spotted lips.

The next morning, I was in the midst of eating a delightful continental breakfast, when I absentmindedly looked out the window and discovered that the ditch bank about ten yards away was thick with a *Spiranthes* species. I immediately gulped down the rest of my orange juice and ran to get my camera. The plants turned out to be *Spiranthes vernalis.*

All of the photographs in this chapter came from that one location, showing how variable this species can be. Some of the flowers had orange spots on the lip, while other flowers had the typical cream-colored strip down the center of the lip. Most of the flowers were loosely spiraled, but some spirals were tight. What a spectacular location!

Once I was able to examine the plants, I knew right off that they were *S. vernalis* by closely examining the tiny hairs on the flowers and the stem. This species has tiny articulated, pointed hairs and is the only *Spiranthes* species to exhibit this characteristic. All of the other *Spiranthes* species with hairs have capitate hairs—each hair has a little ball or club on the end of it. Of course, the orange spots on the lips of one of the plants were also a giveaway, since *S. vernalis* is the only *Spiranthes* species that exhibits this particular characteristic.

This species is also quite hardy and vigorous. The stems are thick and sturdy, unlike those of some of its cousins. When in flower, there are several grasslike leaves at the base of the plant. More than a few of the state's *Spiranthes* species have leaves that are withered at bloom time.

My encounter with *S. vernalis* was a great experience, since I had not previously photographed this species, nor studied it up close. It was an unexpected surprise. There is a saying among orchid enthusiasts that rings true: Orchids are where you find them.

Tight spiral of flowers with an opaque, cream-colored strip centered in each lip.

NOTES:

Crane-fly Orchid

Tipularia discolor (Pursh) Nuttall

Genus: Tipularia—From Latin "Tipula," referring to the generic name of the crane fly.

Species epithet: discolor—From Latin, meaning "two colors," referring to the two colors of the winter leaf: dull green on the top and magenta purple underneath.

Description: This orchid has a cluster of thirty to forty green and purplish brown flowers on a thin, leafless stem that is about fifteen to eighteen inches tall. The flowers, which have narrow sepals and petals, are about one-half to three-fourths inches wide. The lip is about the same size as the petals but narrows into a crook at the tip. The column is a bright lime green.

When in flower, the solitary leaf is withered. But in midwinter, the leaf is the easiest way to recognize the plant; it is dull green on the top and magenta purple underneath.

In flower: Mid-July to mid-August.

Habitat: All types of woods.

Range: Reported from almost all of the counties in the state.

Pollinators: Ants and bees.

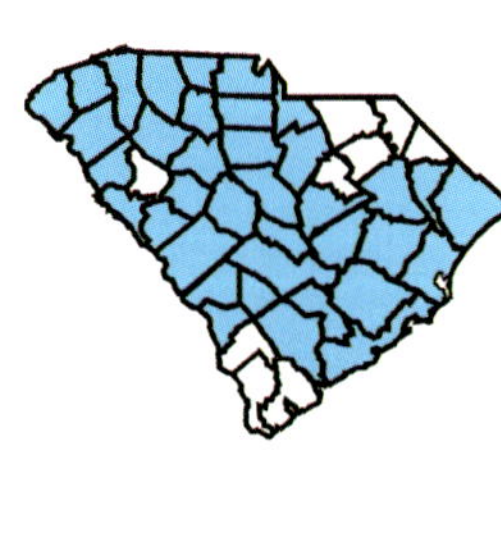

Mid-July to mid-August is the perfect time to view the bloom of the crane-fly orchid. You just have to know where to look for them. The best way to find these elusive plants is to do some midwinter scouting in the woods. Look for scattered clusters of dull green leaves about three inches long and an inch wide. Check the underside of the leaf. It should be a deep magenta purple, which is a dead giveaway for this plant. When you find the leaf, mark its location. It will wither in the spring quite a while before the bloom stalk emerges.

It is one of only two orchids found in South Carolina that has a winter leaf but no leaf when it blooms. The other orchid that exhibits this characteristic is the puttyroot orchid *(Aplectrum hyemale)*. Its leaf is generally much larger and exhibits striking white parallel veining over the entire length of the leaf, which is blue green underneath.

Underside of the leaf of a crane-fly orchid showing the striking color difference.

The flowers of the crane-fly orchid are unusual. The narrow sepals and petals are brownish green to purple, while the column is a bright, almost fluorescent, lime green. The flower is said to look like a crane fly, hence the common name. Each flower supports a long, thin spur that curves down behind the petals.

The bloom stalk is about fifteen to eighteen inches tall, and the loosely spaced flowers stand well away from the stem. Given its subdued colors, thin stem, and preference for dark woods, it is easy to see why this cryptic orchid is hard to spot during its midsummer bloom.

The loose arrangement and subdued colors of its flowers camouflage this species in the deep woods.

NOTES:

Three Birds Orchid
Nodding Pogonia

Triphora trianthophora (Swartz) Rydberg ex Britton

Genus: Triphora—From Latin, meaning "three-bearing," possibly referring to the three green ridges on the lip of the flower.

Species epithet: trianthophora—From Latin, meaning "bearing three flowers," referring to the three flowers sometimes produced on each inflorescence.

Description: The tiny half-inch flowers appear at the apex of a succulent green to reddish green stem. The plants are about four to eight inches tall and have several broadly ovate or heart-shaped leaves. Each flower has petals and sepals that are similar in size and shape and a white lip that sports a crest of three parallel sets of green or yellow green bristles. The petals and sepals may be pure white or white tipped with pink or purple. The flowers quickly fade and are replaced by drooping, green seed pods.

The plants usually bloom when the temperature decreases by ten degrees or more. Within twenty-four to forty-eight hours of this temperature change, the flowers begin to open and remain open for just a few hours.

In flower: Late July to late August.

Habitat: Dry to damp, very acidic woods that are rich in leaf litter.

Range: Found both in the northern mountains and along the coastal plain.

Pollinators: Small bees.

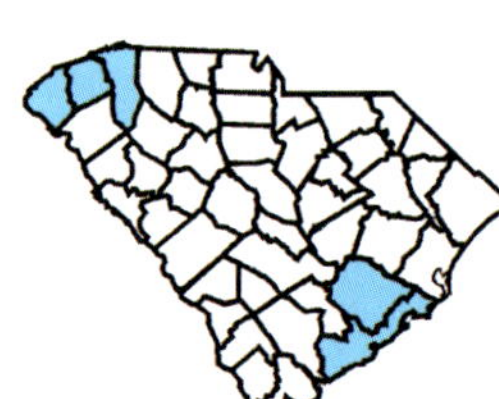

Some people are just lucky. When they go out to look for a rare orchid, they find it on the first attempt. Others, like me, have to try and try again until fate finally smiles.

Actually, finding the three birds orchid is not as big a problem as it might seem. The plants are "creatures of habit." They prefer a damp to dry, very acidic soil. A favorite place that I look for these plants is under the spreading limbs of eastern hemlock *(Tsuga canadensis)* trees or around sandstone outcrops.

The problem associated with finding blooming plants, however, is unique among North American terrestrial orchids. Three birds orchids bloom only when certain strict conditions are met. Sometime in August, they will complete a bloom cycle when the ambient temperature decreases by about ten or more degrees. Strangely, they don't bloom immediately, but wait twenty-four to forty-eight hours. Whether it is the actual drop in temperature that induces flowering or some other more subtle factor associated with this temperature change, experts are not sure.

A common view of Triphora trianthophora, *unless you happen to hit the date and time just right.*

Added to this peculiarity is the fact that the flowers stay open for only about six hours, usually from about 11:00 A.M. to 5:00 P.M. So, if you are not in the right place at the right time, you won't be able to appreciate these tiny beauties in their full glory.

This orchid is most commonly seen with full buds (pictured on the left) or with hanging seed pods (pictured on the right). Looking at the picture on the left, it is not possible to say with any accuracy whether the flowers will open the next day or two to three weeks later. Of course, if you are late and miss the bloom, then you

Seed pods on a group of plants that bloomed weeks before this picture was taken.

NOTES:

will probably see the plant loaded with withered flowers or drooping seed pods.

Some plants produce more than one cycle of buds. It is not unusual to find freshly opened flowers, withered flowers, and seed pods on the same plant.

Though the challenge might seem insurmountable, the delicate three birds orchid provides the orchid enthusiast a wonderful treat.

Appendix A: The Environmental Challenge

The greatest menace facing wildflowers in general and wild orchids in particular is loss of habitat. A major cause of this loss is the draining of wetlands or the building of houses and shopping centers in areas that were once the realm of orchid communities. Other more subtle factors also threaten the state's orchid species.

A high percentage of South Carolina's woods and forests that harbor our orchid species were accustomed to periodic burning, whether from naturally occurring electrical storms or from fires set intentionally by man. Realizing the benefits inherent in such an activity, many of our early ancestors frequently burned the land. They were keenly aware that periodic burning benefits plant and animal communities.

The primary benefit of periodic burning is to create open space by removing existing vegetation. Certain species, such as certain orchid species, quickly become established in the unoccupied habitat. Over time, other colonizing plants invade and outcompete early pioneer plants for available resources, such as light and nutrients, eliminating them from the habitat. Fortunately, these first plants occupy the site long enough to grow and reproduce.

Competition with introduced nonnative species also endangers our native orchid species. Most of our orchid species do not compete well with the more aggressive nonnative woody shrubs and fast-growing grasses and vines that have been introduced into the state. When these plants sprout, even after a prescribed burn, and are allowed to continue to mature, these aggressive plants will soon outgrow the slower growing orchid species. If these successional conditions continue over a long period of time, the orchids may not be able to come back in a particular area.

Another challenge for wildflower communities is presented by the practice of forest monoculture, which is used by large lumber companies, especially in the southeast. Land that once supported large wildflower communities is cleared and planted with trees in very compactly spaced rows. These monoculture forests do not allow room for any other plants to thrive. When these forests mature, heavy equipment is often brought in to harvest the "crop," causing considerable damage to the land and adjoining streams. After the harvest and before the replanting, the land is sometimes treated with herbicides, thereby killing all growing plants, including orchid species.

Even the weather plays a small part in the wild orchids' demise. Late frosts and dry spring and summer seasons will stunt plant and flower production. If a particular population of orchids is initially very small, it may disappear entirely, but usually it can recover after a few years of adverse weather conditions. After all, these weather cycles have been occurring for millennia.

Couple nature's challenges with habitat destruction by humans, which is accruing at an alarming rate, and it is easy to see why some scientists and plant enthusiasts are not encouraged for the long-term survival of many wildflower communities.

What can be done? Well, there are a few things that you can do to make sure South Carolina's orchid species and other wildflowers are available for future generations:

1. **Join and support a local nature or wildflower organization.** Through your active participation in a local environmental organization, you will not only help the organization accomplish its goals, but also increase your knowledge of the state's bountiful natural treasures. One excellent organization is the South Carolina Native Plant Society. This organization has chapters covering all areas of the state.

2. **Contact your local and state representatives when issues arise concerning protection of wetlands or other sensitive areas.** This also includes proposed widening of roadways through environmentally sensitive areas. You may be surprised to know that every personal contact is actually seen to represent many hundreds of constituents.

3. **Read, read, read! Buy a good nature book about a geographic region or about plants of special interest to you.** Your community library or neighborhood bookstore are both great places to begin the search. The Internet also provides a wealth of information when you use any of the commonly available online search engines.

4. **Get out into the woods, swamps, and meadows and become more familiar with your favorite plants.** There are many places in the state that perfectly fit this purpose. They are called heritage preserves. These special tracts were established to protect unusual plant and animal communities, and they can be found all over the state. I visit a number of heritage preserves on a regular basis during different times of the year just to see some of the special orchids and wildflowers that are found there. To learn more about South Carolina's heritage preserves, contact the South Carolina Department of Natural Resources.

Appendix B: Taxonomic Analysis of the Orchid Family

Subfamily	Tribe	Subtribe	Genus
Cypripedioideae	—	—	*Cypripedium*
Epidendroideae	Arethuseae	Arethusinae	*Arethusa*
	"	Bletiinae	*Calopogon*
	"	"	*Hexalectris*
	Calypsoeae	—	*Aplectrum*
	"	—	*Corallorhiza*
	"	—	*Tipularia*
	Cymbidieae	Eulophiinae	*Pteroglossaspis*
	Epidendreae	Laeliinae	*Epidendrum*
	Malaxideae	—	*Liparis*
	"	—	*Malaxis*
	Neottieae	Listerinae	*Listera*
	Triphoreae	—	*Triphora*
Orchidoideae	Cranichideae	Cranichidinae	*Ponthieva*
	"	Goodyerinae	*Goodyera*
	"	Sipranthinae	*Spiranthes*
	Orchideae	Habenariinae	*Gymnadeniopsis*
	"	"	*Habenaria*
	"	"	*Platanthera*
	"	Orchidinae	*Galearis*
Vanilloideae	—	Pogoniinae	*Cleistes*
	—	"	*Isotria*
	—	"	*Pogonia*

* South Carolina species only; based on genetic sequence analysis (Cameron et al., 1999)

Glossary

ACUMINATE: tapering into a slender point

ACUTE: ending in a point

ANTHER: the pollen-bearing portion of a stamen

ANTHESIS: the period during which a flower is open

APOMIXIS: embryo development without fertilization by pollen

APPRESSED: lying flat against another structure

BOG: a type of wetland whose surface is organic (peaty) and whose water is highly acidic; bogs have a high water table maintained directly by rain and snow

BRACT: a modified leaf usually on or below the stalk of a flower or branch of the inflorescence

CAPITATE: forming a head; capitate hairs refers to hairs with ball-like tips

CAPSULE: the matured seedpod, splitting when ripe and containing more than one seed

CAUDICLE: the narrow, tail-like stalk of a pollinium

CHASMOGAMOUS: with fully open, sexual flowers

CILIATE: fringed with hairs on the margin

CIRCUMNEUTRAL: a chemical condition of water or soil that is neither acidic nor alkaline

CLEISTOGAMOUS: having closed flowers that usually self-pollinate

COLUMN: the structure in an orchid that has both anthers (male) and pistil (female) combined into a single element

CONNIVENT: converging but not fused

CORM: an enlarged, fleshy base of a stem

COROLLA: the petals taken together as a whole

CRENULATE: with very small rounded teeth on the margin; scalloped

CRESTED: bearing an elevated appendage or protruding fringes

DISJUNCT: species that are growing far from their usual range

DISTAL: farthest point from attachment

DORSAL: of leaves, bracts, and floral parts, the outer or back side

ENDEMIC: native or confined to a restricted area

ENDOSPERM: tissue within the seed that provides nutrition to the growing embryo

ENTIRE: having a continuous uninterrupted margin without lobes or teeth

EPHEMERAL: short-lived; transitory

EPIPHYTIC: growing on or attached to another plant (supported by tree limbs) but not parasitic

EROSE: having an eroded or jagged margin

FEN: a type of wetland that accumulates peat deposits; less acidic than bogs, deriving most of its water from groundwater rich in minerals

FILIFORM: threadlike

FLATWOODS: any low-lying dry timber lands; such as level pinelands whose characteristic tree is the longleaf pine *(Pinus palustris)*

FUGACIOUS: referring to plant parts; falling away or fading very early

GLABROUS: smooth; without hairs

GLAUCOUS: with a whitish, waxy coating

HABIT: the way a plant grows

HABITAT: where a plant grows

HERBARIUM: a collection of pressed and dried plants prepared for permanent preservation, systematically arranged

HYBRID: offspring of two genetically different individuals belonging to different genera, species, or other taxonomic groups

INFLORESCENCE: the arrangement of flowers or flowering branches, perhaps involving bracts but not foliage or leaves

LABELLUM: the lip of an orchid flower

LANCEOLATE: lance-shaped, several times longer than wide, tapering at both ends

LIP: the modified third petal of an orchid flower

MARSH: a tract of wet or periodically inundated level and treeless land, having a mucky soil and covered mostly with grasses and sedges

MEADOW: a tract of moist (not wet) land characterized by grasses and wildflowers, but without trees or shrubs

MYCORRHIZA: a relationship between plant root cells and fungi; in orchids the relationship is with seeds or roots

MYCOTROPIC: totally dependent upon association with a fungus

NECTARY: a portion of the lip (in orchids) that secretes nectar

NONRESUPINATE: with the lip uppermost

OBLANCEOLATE: lance-shaped, but broadest above the middle and tapering toward the base

OVARY: the lower ovule-bearing part of a pistil; generally capable of forming fruit (seeds)

PANDURATE: fiddle-shaped

PARASITE: a plant that grows on and derives part or all of its nourishment from another plant

PERIANTH: collective term for the petals and sepals on a flower

PETAL: one of the inner floral leaves, including the lip

PETIOLE: the portion of the leaf that connects to the stem

PISTIL: the female organ of a flower, consisting of the stigma, style, and ovary

POLLEN: the grains or mass of grains shed from anthers and normally deposited on the stigma

POLLINARIUM: the pollinium with its caudicle, stipe, and viscidium
POLLINIUM: a coherent mass of pollen
POSTERIOR: lower or rear
PROXIMAL: the inner or closer point to attachment
PSEUDOBULB: thickened or swollen stem usually at the base of a plant; in terrestrial orchids, may be above or below ground
PUBESCENT: covered with short, downy-soft hairs
RACEME: an unbranched, indeterminate inflorescence with stalked flowers; generally, the flowers open from the base to the tip
RANK: the arrangement of flowers in an inflorescence in one or several rows of flowers, seen in the genus *Spiranthes*
REFLEXED: turned downwards or backwards
RESUPINATE: twisted 180 degrees, as in some orchids, which have the lip lowermost, because the flower rotates or turns during development
RHIZOME: horizontal, underground stem
ROSTELLUM: a little beak; the part of the column that contains the stigmatic surface to which the pollen adheres
RUNNER: see stolon
SAPROPHYTE: a plant that lives off decaying organic matter, usually lacking chlorophyll
SAVANNAH: a level grassy plain with scattered trees, supporting numerous flowering herbs and low shrubs, usually containing a fluctuating water level
SECUND: having flowers all on one side of the stem
SEPAL: one of the outer flower structures
SPATULATE: shaped like a spatula, oblong with a narrowed base
SPECIES: an aggregate of individuals that share common characteristics and can interbreed
SPHAGNOUS: referring to *Sphagnum* moss
SPIKE: an unbranched inflorescence with unstalked flowers
SPUR: a slender tubular or saclike structure usually formed at the base of the lip and often containing nectar
STIGMA: the uppermost portion of the pistil, which receives the pollen
STIPE: in orchids, the stalk that connects a pollinium with the viscidium
STOLON: a basal branch rooting at a node, commonly giving rise to new individual plants
STYLE: the portion of a pistil that rises from the ovary and supports the stigma
SWAMP: a tract of land, which is seasonally dry or inundated and dominated by trees and shrubs
SYMPATRIC: occurring together in the same geographic area
TAXONOMY: the systematic classification of plants or animals
TERRESTRIAL: living on or in the ground

TUBER: an enlargement of an underground stem or root tip
TUBERCLE: a small, rounded prominence
TYPE SPECIMEN: a specimen or individual designated as type of a species or lesser group and serving as the final criterion of the characteristics of that group
UNDULATE: wavy
VARIETY: a taxonomic rank below subspecies; minor characteristics that separate varieties from species or subspecies
VENTRAL: of leaves, bracts, and floral parts, the inner or upper side
VISCIDIUM: the sticky material attached to the pollinium, usually produced by the rostellum
VOUCHER: an annotated sheet of paper that has an attached plant specimen and contains valuable written details, such as scientific name, place of origin, and date of collection; usually cataloged and located in a herbarium
WHORL: the arrangement of leaves, petals, sepals, or other flower parts all coming from the same point on the axis in a circular pattern

Bibliography

Batson, Wade T. *Wild Flowers in the Carolinas*. Columbia: University of South Carolina Press, 1987.

Bentley, Stanley L. *Native Orchids of the Southern Appalachian Mountains*. Chapel Hill: University of North Carolina Press, 2000.

Brown, Paul M., and Stan Folsom. *Wild Orchids of the Northeastern United States*. Ithaca and London: Cornell University Press, 1997.

———. *Wild Orchids of Florida: With References to the Atlantic and Gulf Coastal Plains*. Gainesville: University Press of Florida, 2002.

———. *The Wild Orchids of North America, North of Mexico*. Gainesville: University Press of Florida, 2003.

———. *Wild Orchids of the Southeastern United States*. Gainesville: University Press of Florida, 2004.

Cameron, Kenneth M., Mark W. Chase, W. Mark Whitten, Paul J. Kores, David C. Jarrell, Victor A. Albert, Tomohisa Yukawa, Harold G. Hills, and Douglas H. Goldman. "A Phylogenetic Analysis of the Orchidaceae: Evidence from *rbcl* Nucleotide Sequences." *American Journal of Botany* 86 (1999): 208–24.

Correll, Donovan S. *Native Orchids of North America North of Mexico.* Stanford: Stanford University Press, 1978.

Dueck, Lucy, "Wild Orchids in South Carolina—The Story." Aiken: Savannah River Ecology Laboratory, University of Georgia, 2003.

Flora of North America Editorial Committee, eds. *Flora of North America North of Mexico*, Vol. 26. New York and Oxford: Oxford University Press, 2003.

Goldman, D. H. "A new species of *Calopogon* from the Midwestern United States." *Lindleyana* 10(1) (1995): 37–42.

———, and Steve L. Orzell, "Morphological, Geographical, and Ecological Re-evaluation of *Calopogon multiflorus* (Orchidaceae)." *Lindleyana* 15(4)(2000): 237–51.

Gupton, Oscar W., and Fred C. Swope. *Wild Orchids of the Middle Atlantic States*. Knoxville: University of Tennessee Press, 1986.

Hansen, Eric. *Orchid Fever.* New York: Vintage Departures (Random House), 2000.

Justice, William S., and C. Ritchie Bell. *Wild Flowers of North Carolina*. Chapel Hill: University of North Carolina Press, 1968.

Liggio, Joe, and Ann Orto Liggio. *Wild Orchids of Texas*. Austin: University of Texas Press, 1999.

Luer, Carlyle A. *The Native Orchids of Florida*. Brooklyn: New York Botanical Garden, 1972.

———. *The Native Orchids of the United States and Canada Excluding Florida.* Brooklyn: New York Botanical Garden, 1975.

Morris, Frank, and Edward A. Eames. *Our Wild Orchids—Trails and Portraits*. New York: Charles Scribner's Sons, 1929.

Orleans, Susan. *The Orchid Thief.* New York: Ballentine Books, 1998.

Porcher, Richard D. *Wildflowers of the Carolina Lowcountry and Lower Pee Dee.* Columbia: University of South Carolina Press, 1995.

———, and Douglas A. Raynor, *A Guide to the Wildflowers of South Carolina.* Columbia: University of South Carolina Press, 2001.

Radford, Albert E., Harry E. Ahles, and C. Ritchie Bell. *Manual of the Vascular Flora of the Carolinas.* Chapel Hill: University of North Carolina Press, 1968.

Sheviak, Charles J. *Biosystematic Study of the* Spiranthes cernua *Complex*. Bulletin 448, Albany: New York State Museum, 1982.

Smith, S. D., R. S. Cowan, K. B. Gregg, M. W. Chase, N. Maxted, and M. F. Fay. "Genetic Discontinuities Among Populations of Cleistes (Orchidaceae, Vanilloideae) in North America." *Botanical Journal of the Linnean Society* 145 (2004): 87–95.

South Carolina Plant Atlas. <http://cricket.biol.sc.edu/herb/index.html>.

Index

Names in parentheses are not main entries but are mentioned in the text.